Third BBC tv
Top of the Form Quiz Book

compiled by Boswell Taylor

Third BBC tv Top of the Form Quiz Book

compiled by Boswell Taylor

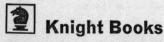 **Knight Books**

the paperback division of Brockhampton Press
by arrangement with the British Broadcasting Corporation

The author would like to express his gratitude for all the help in the making of this book received from Miss Janet Gregory

ISBN 0 340 13483 6

First published 1970 by Knight Books, the paperback division of Brockhampton Press Ltd, Leicester Seventh impression 1974

Printed and bound in Great Britain by Cox & Wyman Ltd, London, Reading and Fakenham

Contents

Questions

General Knowledge 1

1 What is eau-de-Cologne?

2 Where in Edinburgh is the Scott Monument?

3 In camping, what are the 'guys'?

4 In astronomy, what is a 'spectogram'?

5 What did the Amati family teach Antonio Stradivari in the 18th century?

6 At Kirk o' Field what dramatic event took place one February morning in 1567?

7 At the Battle of Waterloo, Wellington commanded the British army. Who commanded the Prussians?

8 What is maté?

9 What are huasos?

10 In fiction, who rode Rosinante?

11 What is a bradawl used for?

12 What name is given to the passages and corridors in ships?

13 What part of our anatomy has bones which makes it sound like a blacksmith's, with anvil, stirrup and hammer?

14 What was the invention which Samuel Colt patented in 1836?

15 What is the shape of a lateen sail?

16 What physical phenomena in various parts of the world are sometimes called 'The Doctor'?

17 What substance in our blood is named after a kind of monkey?

18 What famous organization developed from a pamphlet called *Un Souvenir de Solferino* written by Jean Henri Dunant in 1862?

19 What organization maintains lighthouses round England and Wales?

20 What country celebrates the Feast of St Walpurgis?

The World of Nature

21 What do we call birds and animals that sleep during the day and hunt for their food at night?

22 Reeds grow in marshy ground. What kind of plant is especially suited to desert conditions?

23 Some mammals appear to fly, but what is the only mammal that flies like a bird?

24 A carnivorous animal eats meat. What do we call an animal whose main diet is plant food?

25 For fun we tell the time by the dandelion 'clock', but what is its natural function?

26 Where will you find the spores on a mushroom?

27 What name is given to the process by which water passes from the soil into the roots of plants and up the stems?

28 What do we call the green colouring matter found in plants?

29 In the life cycle of a butterfly, what are the three stages before it becomes an adult butterfly?

30 The male is known as a cob and the female is a pen. What are the young called?

31 The stoat changes its coat in winter. What is the stoat called when it wears its white winter coat?

32 What are the three parts of the jointed body of an insect?

33 What fish is known at various stages of its life as alevin, parr, smolt, grilse and keit?

34 What is the dance of the bees?

35 Saffron is a dye obtained from the flowers of the autumn crocus. What is cochineal obtained from?

36 What does the Mayfly possess that disqualifies it as a true fly?

37 Why might an animal suffer if it attacks a toad?

Myths and Legends

38 Old Father Time is usually shown carrying a scythe. What does Thor the god of thunder carry?

39 According to mythology, Pan was part man and part animal. What animal?

40 Who was the captain of the *Argo* which sailed to Colchis, to get the Golden Fleece?

41 Where did Cerberus live?

42 How did Perseus kill Medusa without turning into stone?

43 In mythology the Greek gods ate ambrosia; what did they drink?

44 What was the name of the nine-headed serpent in Greek mythology who grew two heads every time one was cut off?

45 Mars was the god of war in Roman mythology; who was Somnus?

46 What mythological monster was half-lion and half-eagle?

47 According to legend, Pheidippides ran the first marathon more than two thousand years ago. What was the message he took to the people of Athens?

48 In Greek mythology, who rode Pegasus using a golden bridle?

49 In Greek mythology, who punished Prometheus (by chaining him to Mount Caucasus), and for what reason?

50 Olympus was the home of the Greek gods. What was the home of the Norse gods?

51 One of the seven wonders of the world was the great Colossus of Rhodes. Of which Greek god was this a statue?

52 Who was the Greek hero who was supposed to have swum across the Hellespont every night to visit Hero?

Speed Quiz 1

How many can you get right in TWO minutes?

53 Whose national flag is known as 'The star-spangled banner'?

54 A lamb becomes a sheep; what does a cygnet become?

55 In which country is Magyar the official language?

56 In the story by Daniel Defoe, who had a servant he called 'Man Friday'?

57 What name was given to the writing material that the ancient Egyptians made out of a water plant?

58 Oxford and Cambridge in Britain are to Harvard and what in the United States?

59 In which country are cattle or sheep rounded up by stockmen?

60 At Camelot, King Arthur ruled. Who was his queen?

61 What do we call the molten rock that pours out of volcanoes?

62 Why do bakers put yeast in dough?

63 In the human body, what is another name for the scapula?

64 What important fishing port is approached up the Humber?

65 What is the Hebrew word meaning 'so be it'?

66 The gastric juice of the stomach contains two chief ferments or enzymes. Rennin, is one, what is the other?

67 What is 'Oxfam' short for?

68 Who composed 'The Sleeping Beauty' ballet?

69 Who was the fictional character who fell asleep in the Catskill Mountains for 20 years?

70 How many degrees are there in a triangle?

71 What kind of tree did the jolly swagman sit beside?

72 Earth has one moon; how many moons has Saturn?

Games and Sport 1

73 In what sport do we get a 'half-nelson'?
74 In horse-riding, what is a crupper?
75 In angling, what is a 'gaff'?
76 In British Show Jumping, height separates the horses from the ponies. What is the height limit for ponies?
77 What is another name for the Triple Jump in athletics?
78 In boxing, what is a 'south-paw'?
79 What country played against England in the Final of the 1966 World Cup?
80 What soccer team's home ground is known as Ibrox Park?
81 What soccer team is known as the Potters?
82 Which Rugby Union team is known as the 'All Blacks'?
83 There are three flat races in the Decathlon. One is the 100 metres; what are the other two?
84 Whom do cricketers call 'The Doctor', and whom do footballers call 'The Doc'?
85 In which year did bad weather cause the postponement of more than 300 football matches in England?
86 Denis Compton is an all-round sportsman. For which county did he play cricket, and for which league team did he win an F.A. Cup Medal?
87 Pall Mall is a London street, but what was pall-mall when it was not a street?
88 In cricket, what is a 'stone-waller'?
89 On what ground did Roger Bannister break the '4 minute mile barrier', and in what year?
90 Nurmi was one of the greatest runners of all time. What was his nationality?
91 Name one of the three countries which before 1970 had been successful in winning the World Cup in soccer twice?

Team Quiz 1

92a If a famous person was asked for his autograph, what would he supply?

93a What do we call the place where ice skaters perform?

94a What would be the vocation of a person who regarded it as an honour to be 'hung'?

95a Entomology is the study of insects. What is etymology?

96a What animal provides Laplanders with food and drink and is a means of transport?

97a What is the name of London's chief airport?

98a What island is separated from England by the Solent and Spithead?

99a Into what bay does the river Ganges flow?

100a In days gone by, where did a scullion work?

101a What can a linguist do that most people can't?

102a In fiction, who was the teacher of the Artful Dodger?

103a We have Roman Caesars and Indian Rajahs. In what country was Khedive a title?

104a In which London church were Robert Browning and Elizabeth Barrett married?

105a To be a true Cockney, a Londoner has to be born within the sound of what bells?

106a Who presented the Apothecaries' Society with a 'Physic Garden' in London, now maintained as a botanical garden?

107a What is the link in London's Greenwich Park with Blenheim Palace?

92b If a person was asked for a donation, what would he be expected to supply?

93b What do we call the place where shooting practice is held?

94b What would be the occupation of a person who was 'casting on' and then making a two-inch rib?

95b Astronomy is the science and study of the stars. What is gastronomy?

96b What animal provides the people of Tibet with food and drink and is their chief beast of burden?

97b What is the London borough that once housed the Royal Observatory?

98b What island is separated from Wales by the Menai Strait?

99b Into what sea does the river Indus flow?

100b In the days of highwaymen, where did a tapster work?

101b What can an ambidextrous person do that most people can't?

102b In Shaw's play, who taught Eliza Doolittle?

103b In what country was a bey a ruler?

104b What is the better-known name of the collegiate church of St Peter, in London?

105b What London church is associated with the R.A.F.?

106b What are the legal gardens in London that contain the Royal College of Surgeons with its anatomical museum?

107b What was the former name of London's Regent's Park?

Picture Quiz 1 – Famous People

108 Who are the following famous people?

a

b

c

d

e

f

General Knowledge 2

109 What is a cul-de-sac?
110 In photography, what does an f-number stand for?
111 What event in 1783 caused a 'poet' (or 'contemporary') to write: 'A sight to make surrounding nations stare, A kingdom trusted to a schoolboy's care.'?
112 What is the capital of Chile?
113 In legend, who rode Black Bess?
114 In mathematics, the binary system is based on the number 2. What number is the duodecimal system based on?
115 How many degrees of longitude equal an hour of time?
116 What English king formed the Model Parliament?
117 What sea was referred to as 'Mare Nostrum' by the Romans?
118 What was the novel that Thackeray called 'a novel without a hero'?
119 Who was the author of *Little women*?
120 What is the federal capital of Australia?
121 What is an Egyptian obelisk?
122 The constellation Gemini (the twins) portrays a pair of twins from Greek mythology. What are their names?
123 If a groom referred to a horse's frog, what would he be talking about?
124 Three English kings were killed by an arrow. Who were they?
125 A series of novels by T. H. White was the basis of the Broadway stage play, and subsequently the film *Camelot*. What was the title of T. H. White's quartet?
126 Who was Mr Pickwick's faithful retainer?
127 With which school of philosophy is Jean-Paul Sartre associated?

Science 1

128 What is the chemical element that is common to diamonds, soot and coal?

129 What is a crystal set?

130 What is the metallic element and what is the poisonous gaseous element that combine chemically to form table salt?

131 What solution is used in copper electro-plating?

132 Who was responsible for the famous formula: $E = mc^2$?

133 What is the definition of the word 'laser' (L.A.S.E.R.)?

134 What yellow-green gas is often added to the water in swimming baths to kill any germs in it?

135 What is the smallest known unit of electrical charge?

136 What is the name given to the rays, given off by radioactive substances, that are the most penetrating and most potentially dangerous to man?

137 An 'ampere' is the unit used to measure the rate of flow of an electric current. How did it get its name?

138 What is the name of the belts of radiation that were discovered when satellites began to probe space near the Earth?

139 We know that the sound barrier is one problem for aircraft makers. But what is the 'thermal barrier' that is also a problem in the construction of aircraft?

140 An angle between 180 degrees and 360 degrees we call a reflex angle. What do we call an angle of more than 90 degrees?

141 What is the name of the alkaloid poison contained in tobacco?

142 A Fahrenheit thermometer registers 68 degrees. What would be the reading on a Centigrade thermometer in the same room?

143 If a gear-wheel 2 inches in diameter drives a gear-wheel 12 inches in diameter, what is the ratio of the gears?

Speed Quiz 2

How many can you get right in TWO minutes?

144 Whose national flag features a hammer and sickle?

145 What does a leveret become?

146 In which country is Flemish an official language?

147 Of what Caribbean island is Havana the capital?

148 What is another name for the mandible?

149 Who was the father of our Queen?

150 In *Alice's adventures in Wonderland*, what did the dormouse say was the diet of the three sisters who lived in a well?

151 What would be the nationality of a stamp with the word SUOMI printed on it?

152 What ballroom dance is associated with Vienna?

153 What is the highest British decoration for heroism in combat?

154 What are the very small organisms that cause diseases such as scarlet fever, whooping cough and pneumonia?

155 What is the smallest dog in the world?

156 You know who went hunting for the snark; who is hunting the quark?

157 If a person is canonized, what does he officially become?

158 What sign of the Zodiac is represented by a pair of scales?

159 What was the religious faith of William Penn who founded the American state of Pennsylvania?

160 What British coin ceased to be currency in January 1961?

161 What is measured in *phons and decibels*?

162 What special day is celebrated on 14 February?

163 What is the name that we usually give to the building called the *Rathaus* in Germany?

Quotations 1

164 Who is supposed to have said, *'L'Angleterre est une nation de boutiquiers'*? (England is a nation of shopkeepers.)

165 The following verse comes from a 19th-century translation of a famous poem. What is the poem, and who was the translator?

'A Book of Verses underneath the Bough,
A Jug of Wine, a Loaf of Bread – and Thou
 Beside me singing in the Wilderness –
Oh, Wilderness were Paradise enow!'

166 'I have known him come home to supper with a flood of tears, and a declaration that nothing was now left but a jail; and go to bed making a calculation of the expense of putting bow-windows to the house, "in case anything turned up," which was his favourite expression.'

Whom is the writer describing?

167 The following quotation from Macaulay's *History of England* relates to one of the Kings of England. Which one?

'He had been, he said, an unconscionable time dying; but he hoped that they would excuse it.'

168 Which famous 19th-century circus proprietor and showman is supposed to have said, 'There's a sucker born every minute.'?

169 The author of the play from which the following quotation comes was born in 1860 in Scotland. Name the play and its author.

'Every time a child says "I don't believe in fairies" there is a little fairy somewhere that falls down dead.'

170 'Guns will make us powerful; butter will only make us fat.' The Nazi who said this during a radio broadcast in 1936 committed suicide in October 1946. Who was he?

171 'I only took the regular course . . . the different branches of Arithmetic – Ambition, Distraction, Uglification, and Derision.'
The author of this quotation was a mathematical tutor and the author of books dealing with geometry and trigonometry. The quotation comes from one of his children's books, for which he is far better known. Who was he?

172 Who said, '*Iacta alea est*' (the die is cast), and on what occasion?

173 Which popular character from children's fiction said of himself, 'I am a Bear of Very Little Brain, and long words Bother me,' and who was his creator?

174 Which British Prime Minister said, during a speech in the House of Commons, 'Victory at all costs, victory in spite of all terror, victory however long and hard the road may be; for without victory there is no survival.', and during which War?

175 Which American literary figure, who was also natural scientist, philanthropist and public servant, wrote the following epitaph for himself?

'The body of
. . . . , printer,
(Like the cover of an old book,
Its contents worn out,
And stript of its lettering and gilding)
Lies here, food for worms!
Yet the work itself shall not be lost,
For it will, as he believed, appear once more
In a new
And more beautiful edition,
Corrected and amended
By its Author!'

General Knowledge 3

176 Who was the author of *The tale of Peter Rabbit* and *The tale of Jemima Puddleduck*?

177 What was the surname of Napoleon the First?

178 If a railwayman referred to a 'frog' on the railways, what would he be talking about?

179 In geography, what does a seismoscope indicate?

180 What recurring physical phenomena are given girls' names to distinguish them?

181 According to tradition, how was Sir Francis Drake occupied and what did he say when the news of the sighting of the Spanish Armada was brought to him?

182 What nation came into being on 14 May 1948, when the British Mandate over its country came to an end?

183 Vermilion is a pigment used in making paint. What colour is it?

184 What was the peninsula which gave its name to the Peninsular War at the beginning of the 1800s?

185 Why might a deltiologist 'wish you were there'?

186 What was the nationality of the first Quisling?

187 Who wears a signet ring which is sometimes called 'the fisherman's ring'?

188 In Hardy's *Far from the madding crowd*, what was the tragic outcome of Boldwood's love for Bathsheba?

189 A person is said to have dichromatic vision. Translate this phrase into everyday terms.

190 What name is given to the law which prevents women from succeeding to a throne?

191 Sir Francis Beaufort was a British admiral with no sea battle associated with his name. In what way is his name perpetuated?

192 In the days when Venice was a republic, what name was given to the chief ruler and magistrate?

193 What is the Minch?

Team Quiz 2

194a How many days are there in the month of March?
195a How many years are there in a decade?
196a What kind of port is a heliport?
197a What does a meteorologist do?

198a In what famous palace is the Sistine Chapel?
199a How many legs has a biped?
200a Vitamin B_1 prevents the disease of beriberi. What prevents the disease of scurvy?
201a What chemical element is represented by the symbol Ag?

202a How does a deathwatch beetle make its eerie tapping noise?
203a What is the special name given to the ornamental screen covering the wall at the back of the altar?
204a In the book *Tom Brown's schooldays*, what famous public school did Tom go to?
205a How often is a General Election held in this country?

206a Which king regained the Hebrides from the Norwegians?
207a What famous battle was won by William Wallace, and in what famous battle was he defeated?
208a In what dramatic way did the rule of King James II i.e. James II of Scotland come to an end?
209a How did Rob Roy get this name?

194b How many days are there in February in a leap year?

195b If a person told you he was a centenarian, what would he be claiming to be?

196b What kind of yacht is a sand yacht?

197b What does a speleologist do?

198b In what famous palace is the Hall of Mirrors?

199b How many legs has an ant?

200b What vitamin is necessary to help bone growth?

201b What chemical element is represented by the symbol Cu?

202b How does a cricket-on-the-hearth make its buzzing noise?

203b In Muslim countries, women are often veiled and kept in the house screened from the sight of strangers. What is this custom called?

204b In the Billy Bunter stories, which school did Billy attend?

205b How long is the term of office of the President of the United States?

206b What was the name of the kingdom established in the mid 800s that led to the formation of present-day Scotland?

207b Who were the Maid of Norway's father and mother?

208b To whom was the book *The Kingis Quair* attributed?

209b How did the Royal House of Stuart get its name?

Picture Quiz 2 — Ships and Boats

210 Who sailed round the world alone in 1966/67, and what was the name of his boat, pictured here?

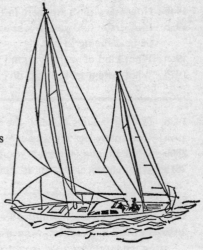

211 What is the name of this boat, used by the Ancient Britons and still in use in Wales?

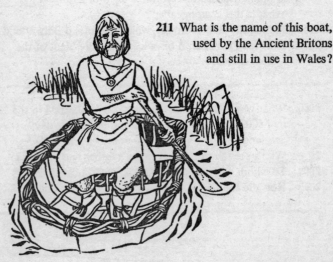

212 This boat is a home.
What is it called?

213 What is the name of this
ship, and why is
she famous?

214 This balsa-wood raft
made a long journey
in 1947. What
is its name?

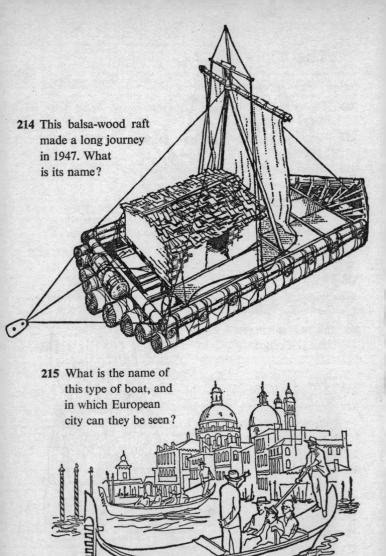

215 What is the name of
this type of boat, and
in which European
city can they be seen?

The Bible

216   The word 'Bible' is derived from the Greek. What does 'bible' mean?

217   What did the serpent persuade Eve to do in the Garden of Eden?

218   How did Judas betray Jesus in the Garden of Gethsemane?

219   What was the total number of years which Jacob had to serve to win Rachel for his wife?

220   How many days, according to Genesis, did God take to create the universe?

221   How many sons did Jacob have?

222   Who owned the tomb in which Jesus was buried?

223   Who was given his freedom when Jesus was condemned?

224   What was the village where Jesus was born?

225   What was the hill on which Jesus was crucified?

226   How did Samson lose his strength?

227   David's greatest friend was a king's son. What was his name?

228   Who was the youngest son of Jacob and Rachel?

229   Who were the two companions of Shadrach who were thrown into the fiery furnace for refusing to worship the golden idol?

230   Who was the eldest son of Adam and Eve?

231   In the New Testament, what was Peter the disciple's first name?

232   In what river was Jesus baptised by John the Baptist?

233   What was the reward that the daughter of Herodias received for her dancing?

234   Modern Protestant versions of the Bible are based on Tyndale's translation. Who was the English reformer who began the first systematic translation of the Bible in the 1380s?

235 The largest planet has the same name as the supreme Roman god. What is it?

236 In which country are the ruins of the ancient city of Troy?

237 When Queen Victoria celebrated her diamond jubilee in 1897, how many years had she been on the throne?

238 For fun the buttercup is held underneath the chin to see if we like butter. In nature, what is the purpose of the brightly coloured petals of the buttercup?

239 What food is associated with Chelsea and Bath?

240 Who was the Moslem warrior who defied the Christian knights in the Third Crusade?

241 In World War I, what was the new weapon that Britain introduced at the Battle of Flers-Courcelette in the Somme Offensive?

242 In Steinbeck's *The grapes of wrath*, what was the state 'flowing with milk and honey' which was their destination?

243 'Mordre woll out', said Chaucer. Who was murdered in the *Prioresses Tale*?

244 Whose statue is the companion piece to Gog in London's Guildhall?

245 Who was the 16th-century Italian statesman who has given his name to a word meaning 'unscrupulous political cunning'?

246 Pemmican was one of the first forms of concentrated food. What is it composed of?

247 What is the common name for the disease called tetanus?

248 The heraldic name for silver is argent. What colour is 'sable'?

249 Who was the mayor of Cologne who became Chancellor of West Germany in 1949 and served until he retired in 1963?

History Miscellany 1

250 What was the name given to the Celtic priests whose sacred symbols were the oak tree and mistletoe?

251 When the Romans built towns in Britain, what was the forum?

252 In the days of King Ethelred II, what was Danegeld?

253 Who was the king who is said to have lost his crown on a gorse bush at the Battle of Bosworth Field?

254 What was the aim of the 'press-gangs' in the days of Nelson?

255 Who became Lord Protector at the end of the British Civil War?

256 Who was Henry the Navigator?

257 Who were the Tolpuddle Martyrs?

258 In the 14th century, who were Wycliffe's 'Lollards'?

259 What was the last military invasion of Britain, that took place in 1797?

260 Which were the three original countries who signed a treaty in 1963 agreeing not to test nuclear weapons in the atmosphere, in outer space, or under water?

261 Iraq was once part of Mesopotamia which means 'between two rivers'. What are the two rivers?

262 How did the 'Flanders Mare' help to bring down Thomas Cromwell, Earl of Essex?

263 What was the Court which met without jury in King Henry VII's palace of Westminster?

264 Canterbury Pilgrims visited the tomb of St Thomas; the Pilgrim Fathers landed in America; where did the leaders of the 'Pilgrimage of Grace' end up?

265 The 1783 Treaty of Paris ended the American War of Independence. What war did the 1856 Treaty of Paris end?

266 What was the name of the hill defended by King Harold against the Norman invaders?

Team Quiz 3

267a   What race of people are supposed to live in igloos?

268a   In what city is the famous Louvre?

269a   In which country is Peking?

270a   In the world of nature, what lives in an eyrie?

271a   What port is built at the mouth of the river Taff?

272a   What great river links Austria to the sea?

273a   What is Portland Bill?

274a   What name is given to the stormy belt of ocean between latitudes 40° and 50° south?

275a   What bird successfully evades domestic responsibilities and whose name is sometimes used to describe a silly person?

276a   What does the saying 'beggars can't be choosers' mean?

277a   The official scale of the Centigrade thermometer is named after the Swedish astronomer who developed it. What is his name?

278a   What was the family name of these famous Florentine relatives: Cosimo, Lorenzo and Catharine?

279a   Which was the first public railway to use steam engines?

280a   Who was the member of Parliament who was the first victim of a railway accident?

281a   Ermine Street was a famous Roman road. Which two cities were the termini?

282a   Who was the road builder who constructed wonderful roads despite a serious physical handicap?

267b What race of people used to live in wigwams?

268b In which city is the famous Kremlin?

269b In which country is Calcutta?

270b In the world of nature, what lives in a drey?

271b What port is built at the mouth of the river Wear?

272b What great river links Switzerland to the North Sea?

273b What is Scapa Flow?

274b What name is given to low pressure calms round the equator?

275b In Britain what bird should try to be elusive on 12 August and whose name as a verb means 'to grumble'?

276b Why would you be foolish to 'put all your eggs in one basket'?

277b Barometers that contain no liquid at all have a special name. What is it?

278b What was the family name of these famous brothers and their sister: Osbert, Sacheverell and Edith?

279b Four steam locomotives competed in the famous Rainhill Trials that took place near Liverpool in 1829. Can you name two?

280b Who was the great railway engineer who was known as the Founder of Railways?

281b The Great North Road is classified A1. What are the common names of two of the following roads: A2, A3 and A5?

282b Who was the road builder, the son of a shepherd, who constructed the Menai Strait Suspension Bridge?

Music and Song

283 What is the name for plays set to music which comes from the Latin word meaning 'works'?

284 In the three main ranges of women's voices, soprano is the highest and contralto is the lowest. What comes in between?

285 In men's voices, tenor is the highest of the three main ranges, and bass is the lowest. What comes in between?

286 What are virginals?

287 What is an organ stop?

288 In the popular song, what was the job of the 'Forty-niner' who loved his darlin' Clementine?

289 What instrument is associated with Semprini?

290 If Yehudi Menuhin and Jacqueline du Pré were appearing at the same concert, what instruments would you expect them to be playing?

291 One of Chopin's compositions is a *berceuse*. What is a *berceuse*?

292 The Promenade Concerts are held annually at the Royal Albert Hall in London. Who founded these concerts, and in what hall were they first performed?

293 A dulcimer is a musical instrument. How is it played?

294 What is a sonata?

295 Some of Schubert's compositions are called *Lieder*. What are *Lieder*?

296 What do we call the leading lady singer in an opera?

297 Which psalm is known as 'The cantate'?

298 What is meant by the term *messa di voce*?

299 How did the dance called *tarantella* get its name?

300 What American bandmaster composed so many musical marches that he was known as the 'March King'?

Who am I?

To be read aloud
This is a 'Who am I?' set with facts about a person, living
or dead, historical or legendary. If you know who it is
after the first fact is given to you, you score 3 points;
after the second fact, 2 points; after the third fact, 1 point.

---

301 (i) The youngest of several children, I was left fatherless
at the age of two. I served as a barman in my mother's
public house. However, I became a servitor in Pembroke
College, Oxford. (ii) I became a deacon and followed
John Wesley to Georgia. I made seven visits altogether
to America and went on many preaching tours
throughout the United Kingdom. (iii) I preached my
first sermon in the Crypt church in Gloucester in 1736.

302 (i) I am a British nuclear physicist who was born in
Lancashire in 1897. (ii) I became director of research at
Harwell Atomic Energy plant in 1946 and held the post
of Master of Churchill College from 1959. (iii) I won
the Nobel prize in 1951 with Ernest Walton for being
the first to split atoms artificially.

303 (i) Born in Queensland, Australia, I am a tennis player
who made a clean sweep of the men's Australian,
French, United States and Wimbledon titles in 1962.
(ii) I won the men's singles title at Wimbledon in 1969.
(iii) I turned professional in 1963 and am regarded as
the world's foremost tennis champion.

304 (i) I was born on 27 November 1921 in Uhrovec in
Western Slovakia. (ii) I became Secretary of my country's
Communist party on 5 January 1968. (iii) My reforms
as party leader met with Soviet disapproval, and I lost
my office.

305 (i) Born in 1857, I was a Swedish doctor and author. (ii) I served as Royal Physician until I retired to the Isle of Capri. (iii) I wrote an autobiography *The Story of San Michele*.

306 (i) I was born in 1872 near Trelleck, Wales, and have made my name as a mathematician, a philosopher, and as a sociologist. (ii) I received the Nobel Prize for literature in 1950. (iii) I led pacifist moves in the '60s, to ban nuclear weapons.

307 (i) I was given the name of Herbert Ernst Karl Frahm when I was born in Lubeck in Germany. I changed my name when I left Germany. (ii) I became governing Lord Mayor of Berlin in 1957. (iii) As leader of the Social Democratic Party, I became Chancellor of Germany in 1969.

308 (i) A Russian novelist, I was born in Moscow in 1890. (ii) In 1922 a book of my poetry was published with the title *My sister, life*. (iii) I won the 1958 Noble Prize for Literature with my book *Dr Zhivago*.

309 (i) A British physicist, I was born in Wigton, Cumberland, in 1862. (ii) I shared the Nobel Prize in physics with my son for research on the structure of crystals. (iii) Also with my son I developed the X-ray spectrometer and discovered a great deal about the atomic arrangement in crystals.

310 (i) A Spanish novelist, I was born in Valencia in 1867. (ii) I wrote a novel called *Blood and sand*. (iii) A famous film was made from my novel – *The Four Horsemen of the Apocalypse*.

311 (i) I was born on 4 December 1892 in El Ferrol in the province of Galicia. (ii) I was commander-in-chief of the Nationalists of my country, and gained victory on 1 April 1939. (iii) I was born Francisco Bahamonde, but as dictator of my country I am known by another name.

312 (i) Born in Birmingham, I am a tennis player who was beaten by Mrs King in the 1967 Wimbledon championship Final. (ii) I had my revenge when I won the Singles Championship at Wimbledon in 1969. (iii) I was voted Sportswoman of the Year in 1969.

313 (i) Born in 1893, I was a poet in the First World War. (ii) I was killed one week before the Armistice in 1918. (iii) One of my poems begins, 'I too saw God through mud'.

314 (i) I was born on 25 January 1929 in Atlanta, United States, the son of a Baptist minister. (ii) I received the Nobel Prize for peace in 1964. (iii) I preached 'non-violent resistance' to achieve full civil rights for negroes in America.

315 (i) I was born in 1919 in Montreal and attended the Jesuit College there, and studied at Harvard, the University of Paris, and the London School of Economics. (ii) I was a law professor in Montreal before I entered politics and became leader of the Liberal Party in Canada. (iii) I became Prime Minister of Canada in 1968.

316 (i) A German playwright, I was born in Augsburg in 1898. (ii) In 1922 I wrote *Baal*, but achieved greater success six years later with *The threepenny opera*. (iii) Among my other successes are *Mother Courage* and *The Caucasian Chalk Circle*.

Speed Quiz 3

How many can you get right in TWO minutes?

317 What would be the nationality of a stamp with the word SVERIGE printed on it?

318 What breed was known as the royal dog of China?

319 What does a parasol protect a person against?

320 When 'flora' describes plant life, what word is used to describe animal life?

321 What name do we give to the fruit of the bramble?

322 What do we call the line that divides a circle into a semi-circle?

323 What is the name of the famous ancient university in Paris?

324 In the Old Testament, what man was famous for his patience?

325 In Muslim countries, who calls the faithful to prayer?

326 In Charlotte Brontë's novel, whom did Jane Eyre marry?

327 In *Hamlet*, who was Ophelia's father?

328 In Britain, if a traffic light shows amber alone, what is the next light?

329 What is a Kerry Blue?

330 What is the latitude of the North Pole?

331 What useful metal is obtained from cinnabar?

332 In Italian comedy, who is Harlequin's sweetheart?

333 What kind of vessel was a U-boat?

334 What country is sometimes known as *Cymru*?

335 The first name of Mr Onassis, the Greek-born ship-owner, is the same as the name of an ancient Greek philosopher. What is it?

336 According to Alfred Noyes, when should we go down to Kew?

337 What part of the plant is used to get 'liquorice'?

Shakespeare

338 In which Shakespeare play do we hear a song which starts, 'Where the bee sucks, there suck I', and who is the singer?

339 In *A Midsummer Night's Dream*, who is Oberon's elfin or fairy messenger?

340 Who are Titania's four fairies?

341 Who speaks the epilogue to *The Tempest* beginning, 'Now my charms are all o'erthrown'?

342 Who is the sleep-walking villainess who recalls a crime with these words: 'Out, damned spot! Out, I say!'? And who was murdered?

343 Who is the wicked uncle who married Hamlet's mother?

344 Who becomes King of Scotland at the end of *Macbeth*?

345 In *The Merchant of Venice*, how much did Antonio borrow from Shylock, and for how long?

346 If Romeo and Juliet had surnames, what would they be?

347 In *Othello*, the first act is set in Venice. Where are the scenes set for the rest of the play?

348 Who was Othello's predecessor in the government of Cyprus?

349 In *Hamlet*, who was King of Denmark?

350 In *As you like it*, who is the clown?

351 What was the treasure sent by the Dauphin as a gift to King Henry V?

352 In *Antony and Cleopatra*, how does Cleopatra die?

353 Who disguised herself as Balthazar, doctor of laws, to defend the Merchant of Venice against Shylock?

354 Robin Goodfellow has many aliases. What name does Shakespeare give the little fellow?

355 In *A Winter's Tale*, a statue comes to life. How is this apparent miracle achieved?

Picture Quiz 3 — Buildings

356 This royal castle was the childhood home of the Queen Mother. What is its name?

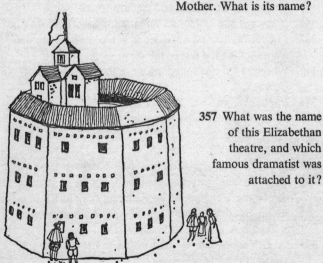

357 What was the name of this Elizabethan theatre, and which famous dramatist was attached to it?

358 Who designed this cathedral, and where is it?

359 What is the name of this famous house, where Queen Elizabeth I received news of her accession?

360 What industry was carried on in these unusual Victorian houses?

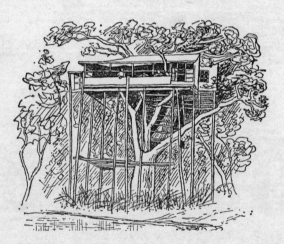

361 Where is this unusual building, and what is it used for?

362   The British Prime Minister has two official titles. The first is 'Prime Minister', what is the other?

363   Who was the queen who defied Suetonius Paulinus when he was the Roman governor of Britain?

364   The planet that orbits farthest from the sun has the same name as the god of the Underworld. What is it?

365   In which country are the ruins of the ancient city of Carthage?

366   Bats produce very high-pitched sounds as they fly. Why?

367   What was the name of the girl who featured in the stories of Robin Hood?

368   In what country are the Cambrian Mountains?

369   What do we measure in 'roods'?

370   What do we call the sacred songs sung by David?

371   What solid geometrical figure does this describe? 'A solid figure, all the points on the surface of which are at the same distance from the centre.'

372   How did Alexander loosen the Gordian Knot?

373   Who was the saint who set up his community on the island of Iona?

374   What is the Parliament of Iceland called?

375   What was the name of the Irish society formed by Arthur Griffiths in 1905 which called itself by the Gaelic words interpreted as either 'ourselves alone' or 'we ourselves'?

376   What was the name of the ideal island which Sir Thomas More claimed was described to him by Ralph Hythlodaye?

377   What was the remarkable venue for the meeting of Napoleon and the Czar of Russia in Tilsit in July 1807?

378   What was the historic operation carried out at the Groote Schuur Hospital in South Africa on 3 December 1967?

Team Quiz 4

379a   In the kitchen, what do you expect to find in a caddy?

380a   What is a monkey puzzle?

381a   If you spelt a word phonetically, what would you be doing?

382a   What is the common characteristic of all rodents?

383a   What is the characteristic feature of a Manx cat?

384a   What is the nationality of a Breton?

385a   King Henry VIII had six wives. His first wife had two husbands – who was her first husband?

386a   Who introduced the 'Special Theory of Relativity' in 1905?

387a   In literature, his friends are Mole, Ratty and Badger. Who is he?

388a   In the book *The house at Pooh Corner* by A. A. Milne, who lived in the House at Pooh Corner?

389a   Edward Lear was fond of sending his nonsense rhyme characters to sea. Who went to sea 'in a beautiful pea-green boat'?

390a   Who is the fictional character who travels through many trials and tribulations to the Celestial City?

391a   Which Welsh lawyer became the chancellor of the exchequer who sponsored the 1911 National Insurance Act?

392a   The river Dee forms the boundary between north Wales and England. Where is its source?

393a   Which Welsh author wrote the play *The corn is green*?

394a   Who built the Britannia Tubular Bridge across the Menai Strait?

379b In sport, what would you expect a caddie to be carrying?

380b What is a Great Dane?

381b If you copied out notes 'verbatim', what would you be doing?

382b What is the characteristic of a 'prehensile' tail?

383b What is the characteristic feature of a Dachshund?

384b What is the nationality of a Sicilian?

385b Josephine was Napoleon's first wife. Who was his second?

386b Who expounded the 'theory of gravity' in 1687?

387b His friends are Athos, Porthos and Aramis. Who is he?

388b In *Nicholas Nickleby* by Dickens, who was the Headmaster of Dotheboys Hall?

389b Who, in an Edward Lear poem, 'went to sea in a sieve'?

390b Who is the fictional character who meets the giants of Brobdingnag?

391b Who was the Welsh coal-miner who ultimately became the Minister of Health and introduced in 1948 the National Health Service?

392b Which is the longest Welsh river entirely in Wales?

393b Which Welsh author wrote the novel *How green was my valley?*

394b Which Cardiff man, well-known for a number of popular musicals, wrote the song 'Keep the home fires burning'?

Games and Sport 2

395 Who is the player in soccer who is sometimes referred to as the 'custodian'?

396 What does the chequered flag signify in motor racing?

397 In what sport might a man call '*touché*'?

398 In what sport are the contestants expected to conform to the Queensberry Rules?

399 What is the usual means of transport on the Cresta Run?

400 In what sport or pastime are 'cues' used?

401 What game is played by the Harlem Globetrotters?

402 Where might you play the game of shinty, and what is the similar game played in England?

403 In what sport are the 'Ashes' played for, and which are the competing countries?

404 Of what country is lacrosse the national summer game?

405 In cricket, how many balls to an over are there in Australia and England?

406 What is the fastest stroke in swimming?

407 In a golf tournament, what is the maximum number of clubs that can be carried in one's bag?

408 In horse-riding, what is the pommel?

409 In what game is a period of play known as a chukker?

410 What is the Eisenhower Trophy?

411 How many numbered segments are there on a darts board?

412 What name is given to the playing objects that are used in 'curling'?

413 When can a player of chess have two moves at once?

414 In round-scoring in amateur boxing, how many marks are assigned to each round?

Poets and Poetry

415 Who was the English poet who wrote a famous poem on his blindness?

416 Who was the English poet who, in his 'Home thoughts, from abroad', wished to be in England now that April's there?

417 What is the next line in this quotation from 'The rime of the ancient mariner'? 'Water, water, everywhere . . .'

418 What are the next few words in this quotation from 'Jabberwocky'? ''Twas brillig, and the slithy toves did gyre . . .'

419 Robert Browning's poem 'Childe Roland to the dark tower came' is based on a song from one of Shakespeare's plays. Which play?

420 Edward Fitzgerald achieved fame with his translation of the work of a Persian poet. What is the title of this poem?

421 What poem by Matthew Arnold is based on the Persian national epic 'Shah Nameh'?

422 What poem is prefaced by the quotation 'Of Brownyis and of Bogillis full is this buke'?

423 What poem by Tennyson begins, 'So all day long the noise of the battle roll'd, Among the mountains by the winter sea;'?

424 Who was the 'Widow of Windsor' to whom Rudyard Kipling addressed one of his Barrack-Room Ballads?

425 What was the famous poem that was first dreamed by the poet and then never finished because of an interruption by a 'man from Porlock'?

426 What poet expressed a premonition in these words: 'When I have fears that I may cease to be, Before my pen has gleaned my teeming brain.'?

Master Brain 1

427 For what purpose does the motor car use ethylene dibromide combined with tetraethyl lead?

428 Who was the famous architect of the restoration period who also became professor of astronomy at Oxford University?

429 What is a 'maiden assize'?

430 The zenith is the point in the heavens directly overhead. What name is given to the opposite or the point directly below?

431 General James Wolfe, the victor of Quebec, was born at Westerham. What British statesman is usually associated with this Kent market town?

432 In photography, some cameras record on the film a view which is slightly different from that seen through the viewfinder. What do we call this difference?

433 Name one of the three gas laws that are combined in the 'Universal Gas Laws'.

434 Baden Powell founded by Boy Scouts; who founded the Boys' Brigade?

435 What was the act that Napoleon did in 1815 in which he compared himself to Themistocles seating himself at the hearth of his enemy?

436 In atomic physics, what is Pu-239?

437 Churchill wrote the *History of the English-speaking peoples*. Who wrote the *Ecclesiastical history of the English nation*?

438 In Shakespeare's *The Tempest*, who is the jester?

439 What was the famous 'gauge dispute' in railway history?

440 What does a tachometer measure?

441 What is the smallest positive whole number that is both the square of a whole number and the cube of the same whole number?

442 Who was the author of the book that Fielding parodied in *Joseph Andrews*?

General Knowledge 6

443 What did the commemorative crown piece struck in 1953 celebrate?

444 If a householder declared that he had been visited by a poltergeist, what kind of visitor would he have had?

445 Of what substance are stalactites and stalagmites in caves mainly composed?

446 If you were given a planchette, what kind of instrument would you have?

447 What is the title of the book with the sub-title 'The preservation of favoured races in the struggle for life'?

448 What country was once known as the cockpit of Europe?

449 Mussolini had his 'Black Shirts' and Hitler his 'Brown Shirts', but who were the 'Red Shirts'?

450 One of the titles of the Sovereign is 'Fidei Defensor' or 'Defender of the Faith'. Which British monarch first earned this title?

451 In the metric system, the kilogram is the standard unit of weight. What is the standard unit of volume?

452 A Turkish statesman began with the name of Mustafa, added the nickname Kemal and was then called in turn Pasha and Ghazi. By what name is this statesman better known?

453 Who or what was 'Roan Barbary'?

454 What was the battle in which the Charge of the Light Brigade was made?

455 What is *poste restante*?

456 What were the Christian names of the three remarkable daughters of the rector of Haworth?

457 What organization has a newspaper called *The War Cry*?

458 In science-fiction appear strange creatures. What is the 'kraken' that John Wyndham wakes?

459 What is this monument, and where is it found?

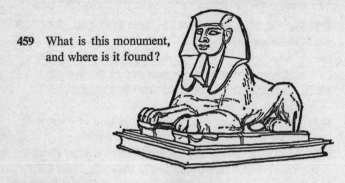

460 Where would these machines be found, and what were they used for?

461 What are these knights doing?

462 What is happening in this picture?

463 What task is this prisoner engaged in?

464 What job are these farm-workers in Stuart times doing?

Team Quiz 5

465a Which king fell asleep and let the cakes burn?

466a Who invented the 'point' system of reading by touch?

467a According to the proverb, what do birds of a feather do?

468a In the study of the atom, what do we call the centre core?

469a According to tradition, in the New Testament who was the author of the First Gospel?

470a In the educational world, what is Oxbridge?

471a In North America, of which river is the Missouri a tributary?

472a A process for making rubber more durable is named after the Roman god of fire and metal-working. What was his name?

473a What insect spreads malaria?

474a Sir Edmund Hillary reached the summit of Everest, but who was in charge of the British expedition?

475a A botanist studies plants, but what does a cytologist study?

476a In detective fiction, who created 'Paul Temple'?

477a What is the connexion between Old Sarum and Salisbury Cathedral?

478a Salisbury is in the Thomas Hardy country. What name did the author use for this part of England?

479a Two of William the Conqueror's sons died in the New Forest. Who were they?

480a How did Prince Richard, son of William I, die?

465b Which king put his throne on the seashore and told the tide not to come in?

466b Who first sent a message by radio across the Atlantic?

467b According to the proverb, what is a bird in the hand worth?

468b In the study of the atom, what do we call the very light particles that orbit round the nucleus?

469b In the New Testament, who wrote the 'Epistle to the Romans'?

470b In the world of fiction, what is Ambridge?

471b In Europe, of which river is the Moselle a tributary?

472b A pain-killing drug was named after the Greek god of dreams. What was his name?

473b What insect spreads the Black Death?

474b Lovell and Anders were the crew of Apollo 8, the first space-craft to orbit the Moon. Who was the commander in charge of the flight?

475b A draftsman draws plans, what does a taxidermist do?

476b In detective fiction, who created 'The Saint'?

477b There is a monument in Salisbury Cathedral which some people maintain is of a 'boy bishop'. What was the ceremony of the 'boy bishop'?

478b What did Thomas Hardy call Salisbury Cathedral?

479b Who were the 'verderers' of the New Forest?

480b How did William Rufus die?

Literature

481 In Aesop's fables, what creature rescued the lion when he was trapped in a net?

482 What is the name of the 'Uncle' who is the teller of stories about Brer Rabbit?

483 In a Dickens novel, who lodged with the Micawbers and was articled to Messrs. Spenlow and Jorkins?

484 Who is the author of *The Forsyte saga*?

485 In a famous novel about the life of a horse, the hero shares the stables with Ginger and Merrylegs. What is his name?

486 Who was the authoress of *Frenchman's Creek*, whose father was a famous actor?

487 Who was the author of 'Ode to the West Wind' whose wife wrote *Frankenstein*?

488 Who was the remorseless French enemy of the Scarlet Pimpernel?

489 Alice went down a rabbit hole. How did Lucy in the first *Narnia* book get to her magic world?

490 What was the nom-de-plume of Eric Arthur Blair, the English novelist and social critic?

491 What was the name adopted by the Polish sailor, born Josef Korzeniowski, who became a British novelist?

492 In Dickens' *Great expectations*, who was Pip's mysterious benefactor?

493 Tennyson and T. H. White, who both wrote about Camelot, acknowledged their indebtedness to *Le Morte d'Arthur*. Who was the 15th century author of this work?

494 What poem by Geoffrey Chaucer has a similar title, and theme, to a play by Shakespeare?

495 What novel by Graham Greene has a title taken from the Lord's Prayer?

496 Who was Don Quixote's faithful retainer?

497 Why do salmon leap?

498 What is the nationality of Corsicans?

499 With what historical character is Domremy in France associated?

500 A pyramid may have a square base. What do we call the pointed solid with a round base?

501 What is the German name meaning 'children's garden' that we have adopted for schools or classes with very young children?

502 In the human body, what is the name given to the fluid that is produced by the lachrymal glands?

503 In fairy tales, who was protected by seven dwarfs?

504 What country would you be in if you paid 40 krone for some porcelain?

505 In Dickens, who was the headmaster of Blimber Academy?

506 If a lepidopterist offered to show you his collection, what would you expect to see?

507 What religious sect were given their nickname by a magistrate because their leader told a court to 'tremble at the word of the Lord'?

508 Why could the ten days from 5 October to 14 October 1582 be known as the 'ten lost days'?

509 Evelyn Waugh wrote *Decline and fall*; who wrote the *History of the decline and fall of the Roman Empire*?

510 What was the name of the world's first wholly commercial communications satellite?

511 Who was the author of *Mein Kampf*, and in what circumstances was it written?

512 The Pied Piper charmed the rats out of Hamelin. What is the name of the river in which they were drowned?

513 In Rudyard Kipling's *Jungle book*, what kind of animal was Shere Khan, the outlaw of the jungle?

Science 2

514 What is the gaseous element that is present in ammonia, laughing gas and dynamite?

515 If deuterium reacts with oxygen, what is the product?

516 You might find ice-cream stored in a box with dry ice. What is dry ice?

517 What is 'fool's gold'?

518 We know the air we breathe contains oxygen, but what is the other gas present in far larger proportions than oxygen?

519 pH is a number used to indicate the strength of an acid or a base. What is the pH of pure water?

520 What is the average atmospheric pressure at sea level in pounds per square inch?

521 What metal has an atomic number of 12 and is mainly obtained from sea water?

522 What metal has an atomic number of 92 and is the main source of atomic energy?

523 In the study of living cells, what do the letters DNA represent?

524 What is the tiny one-celled animal that is sometimes called the slipper animalcule because of its shape?

525 What do we call the point in the orbit of a planet at which the planet is nearest to the sun?

526 Whose gas law can be written: PV = constant?

527 What scientific achievement was known as Project Gemini?

528 What gas is made with the Haber-Bosch Process?

529 What is the chemical name for Glauber's salt?

530 What are Kepler's three laws concerned with?

531 Who discovered natural radioactivity?

532 What name is given to the unit of energy needed to send an electric current of one ampere through a circuit of one ohm resistance?

533 'And behold there was a very stately palace before him, the name of which was Beautiful.' The book from which this comes has been called 'the most beautiful description of Christian experience'. The author, who wrote other books of a similar nature, died in 1688. Who was he, and what was the title of his most popular book?

534 'We present you with this Book, the most valuable thing that this world affords. Here is wisdom; this is the royal Law; these are the lively Oracles of God.' This is spoken during a service which takes place at irregular intervals in London. What is the service, and which book is being presented?

535 Complete this verse, and name the author.
'They dined on mince, and slices of quince,
Which they ate with a runcible spoon;'

536 Who claimed that '*Die Religion . . . ist das Opium des Volkes*' (Religion . . . is the opium of the people)?

537 To which English queen is the following attributed?
'When I am dead and opened, you shall find "Calais" lying in my heart.'

538 Whose description of autumn is this?
'Season of mists and mellow fruitfulness . . .'

539 Which German poet's last words are said to have been 'More Light!'?

540 Which 20th-century English poet wrote these lines?
'Slowly, silently, now the moon
Walks the night in her silver shoon.'

541 Who said: 'Genius is one per cent inspiration and ninety-nine per cent perspiration'?

542 'I saw something nasty in the woodshed' is an oft-repeated sentence in a 20th-century novel which has become something of a classic. Who had the unfortunate experience referred to, and what was the book?

543 The following is an extract from a poem by a 20th-century American poet who lived in, and wrote about, New England. Who was he?

'My apple trees will never get across
And eat the cones under his pines, I tell him.
He only says, "Good fences make good neighbours." '

544 Who is supposed to have said, when dismissing a student, 'You have deliberately tasted two worms and you can leave Oxford by the town drain.'?

545 'I grow old ... I grow old ...
I shall wear the bottoms of my trousers rolled.'
Who is the subject of the poem (which first appeared in 1917) from which these lines are taken, and who was the author (also a publisher)?

546 In the story of the Ancient Egyptians, who was Re?

547 What is the special name given to Tibetan monks?

548 The American industrialist who developed the motor car once said 'History is bunk'. Who was he?

549 An Italian astronomer who was forced to deny that the Earth moves round the Sun is said to have exclaimed 'Yet it does move'. Who was he?

550 Geologists divide the history of the earth into eras. The first era in Precambrian Time is 'Azoic'. What are the other two eras in Precambrian Time?

551 In Greek mythology, Penelope promised to marry the suitor who could do a simple test. What was it?

552 Which prehistoric animal is related to the elephant?

553 What were the 'pump rooms' at Bath and Harrogate?

554 Who was the author of *The death of a salesman*?

555 Name the source of spermaceti, used in ointment.

556 If you accepted wampum from a Red Indian, what would you expect to get?

557 Fort Peck, one of the largest earth-filled dams in the world, controls the waters of which American river?

558 What do we call the morbid dread of wide open spaces?

559 What name is given to the lower house of the Isle of Man Parliament?

560 What name is given to the best known of the Israeli communal settlements?

561 Between which two seas do the Caucasus Mountains lie?

562 What colour does ultramarine describe?

563 In the London-to-Sydney air race, the competitors had to fly a minimum of 10,575 miles. What would be the shortest distance for a race right round the world?

564 Who were the two husbands of Catherine of Aragon?

History Miscellany 2

565 What was the name given to the warring tribes from Scotland against whom the Romans built Hadrian's Wall?

566 When the first Anglo-Saxon kings ruled Britain, what was the Witan or Witenagemot?

567 Who was the son of King Edward III who won his spurs at the Battle of Crécy?

568 Who was President of the United States during their Civil War?

569 According to tradition, how did Nelson receive the signal to retire at the Battle of Copenhagen?

570 In World War II, who was the American President who represented the U.S.A. at the Yalta Conference?

571 What was the sea that separated the conflicting nations in the Punic Wars?

572 Rasputin was a sinister figure in Russian court circles before the First World War. Why was he able to exert such an influence over the Russian royal family?

573 How did Britain acquire a large part of the stock of the Suez Canal?

574 Who was the Italian musician who became the private secretary of Mary, Queen of Scots?

575 What title (by which he was ultimately known) did the Regent give to Sir Arthur Wellesley for his services as a soldier?

576 Who was the last czar of Russia?

577 Two Germans were responsible for the *Communist Manifesto*. One was Engels; the other is better known. Who was he?

578 The bicentenary of the birth of the 'Little Corporal' was celebrated in 1969. Who was the 'Little Corporal'?

579 In World War II, who was known as 'Lord Haw-Haw'?

580 Who was the Spanish adventurer who conquered Peru in the 16th century?

Master Brain 2

581 Politicians have their plans; scientists have their laws. What is Hooke's Law?

582 What was the Marshall Plan that the American Secretary of State proposed after World War II?

583 In which part of the British Isles is a judge known as a 'deemster'?

584 In the bargains made at the Congress of Vienna, what happened to Norway?

585 In the French Revolution, who were the *Mountain* and the *Plain*?

586 In the American Civil War, who were Johnny Reb and Billy Yank?

587 How did Xerxes get his army across the Hellespont in 480 BC?

588 What were the 'Rebecca' Riots in Wales in the 1840s?

589 Where would you be to hear the Lutine Bell rung?

590 These words were uttered on 10 March 1876. Why are they famous? 'Mr Watson, come here. I want you!'

591 Three of King Henry VIII's children succeeded to the throne. Who was the mother of Edward VI, and who was the mother of Elizabeth I?

592 The journey by Jumbo-jet from New York to London takes about 7 hours. What trip takes 27 days 7 hours 43 minutes and 11.5 seconds?

593 What is Kepler's First Law?

594 According to H.G.Wells, where is the One-eyed Man King?

595 Who was Modestine, and who travelled with Modestine in the Cevennes?

596 Simplifying a scientific relationship, deuterium is twice as heavy as normal hydrogen. What is the hydrogen isotope that is three times as heavy?

597 Who was the king who put a price on William the Silent's head?

Speed Quiz 4

How many can you get right in TWO minutes?

598 From what tree do we get the fruit known as conkers?
599 In the Old Testament, what man was famous for his wisdom?
600 With which legendary heroine is Coventry associated?
601 What is carried by aqueducts?
602 Whom did Ben Jonson call 'Sweet Swan of Avon'?
603 What do we call animals that are able to live on land or in water?
604 What name is given to the unit of electrical power?
605 In fairy tales, who invaded the home of Father Bear, Mother Bear and Baby Bear?
606 What name is given to a fertile place in a desert?
607 If a country is holding a plebiscite, what are the people expected to do?
608 If a king abdicates, what does he do?
609 By tradition, what was the badge of favour worn by supporters of the House of Lancaster during the 1400s?
610 Where is Davy Jones' Locker?
611 Whose portrait has become famous as the 'Mona Lisa'?
612 Who was the Italian merchant-explorer whose name was given to America?
613 What is combined chemically with lead to make red lead?
614 What is the official language of Cuba?
615 How many days are there in the religious fasting period known as Lent?
616 What is the name of an Indian elephant keeper and driver?
617 Who or what is 'Black Maria'?

Geography

618 What is the island state of Australia?
619 In which country are criminals tracked by 'Mounties'?
620 For what purpose do many tourists visit the Netherlands in the spring?
621 What is the 'continental shelf'?
622 What mountains form the boundary between Russia (in Europe) and Siberia?
623 What is a 'watershed'?
624 What tiny country, ruled by Prince Franz Josef II, is sandwiched between Austria and Switzerland?
625 In the North American continent, what is divided by the Continental Divide?
626 India and Ceylon border the west of the Bay of Bengal. What are the two countries that border the Bay of Bengal on the north and north-east?
627 What agricultural crop is grown in vast quantities round the city of Sao Paulo?
628 What is the name of the channel that links the Kattegat with the North Sea?
629 The Aswan Dam controls the waters of the river Nile. What famous dam completed in 1959 controls the waters of the river Zambezi?
630 Why is Thailand sometimes called the 'Land of the Yellow Robe'?
631 When it is one o'clock in the afternoon in London, what time is it in Tokyo?
632 What was the British island in the South Atlantic that had to be evacuated in 1961 because of the eruption of a volcano?
633 In what city would you be if you paid 20 kopecks for an ice-cream in Gorki Park?
634 The white cliffs of Dover are of chalk. What is the Rock of Gibraltar made of?

General Knowledge 9

635   Olympic champions receive gold medals. What was the reward for victorious athletes in the days of the Ancient Greeks?

636   In meteorology, what name is given to the feathery, white clouds of ice crystals that form high above all other clouds?

637   In the world of small water creatures, how do flagellates manage to swim?

638   Where in Ireland do thousands of people gather on the last Sunday in July, and why?

639   What was the name of the dog which was the first space traveller?

640   What is the common interest of the men who call at Lincoln's Inn in London?

641   The *Pinta* and *Nina* were two of the vessels in a fleet that set sail in 1492 on an historic voyage. What was the name of the third vessel?

642   What are the White Dwarfs of the sky?

643   Dick Fosbury jumped 7 feet 4¼ inches at the Mexico Olympics; untrammelled by equipment, how high should he be able to jump at the Moon Olympics?

644   Many words begin with 'tele . . .' What does this prefix mean?

645   Who was the famous dancer who was killed when her long scarf was caught in the wheel of a motor-car?

646   In photography, what do the terms 'depth of field' and 'exposure' mean?

647   In science jargon, what 'explosion' can be identified with Enrico Fermi?

648   *Volt* is a scientific term, *volta* a musical one. What is *Upper Volta*?

649   What is the origin of Mark Twain's pen name?

Answers

General Knowledge 1

1   A perfume . . . from Cologne in Germany. Literally = water of Cologne.

2   In Princes Street.

3   Ropes secured at the seams of the tent to enable it to be held to the ground. Sometimes called 'guy lines', they are pegged into the ground and have runners to adjust their length.

4   The photograph of a star's spectrum, showing the various colours in the star's light.

5   How to make violins.

6   Darnley, the husband of Mary, Queen of Scots, was killed when Kirk o' Field was blown up with gunpowder. His body was found at some distance from the house, and it was said that he was strangled when making his escape.

7   Blücher.

8   A kind of tea made from the dried leaves and shoots of a South American plant of the holly family.

9   The cowboy-farmers of Chile.

10 Don Quixote.

11 To make holes in wood . . . originally for brads (small nails).

12 Gangways.

13 The ear. They are three small moveable bones contained in the middle ear.

14 A repeating pistol.

15 Triangular. Used mainly in Mediterranean waters, off the North African coast.

16 Winds, on account of their moderating effect on otherwise unpleasant weather conditions, e.g. Harmattan of West Africa.

17 Rhesus factor (or RH factor).

18 Red Cross. Dunant was a Swiss philanthropist travelling in Italy in 1859 during the Austro-Sardinian War. He saw the battlefield with 40,000 dead or wounded at Solferino. In 1863, delegates from 16 nations met at Geneva and the groundwork for the Red Cross Movement was established.

19 Trinity House Corporation.

20 Germany. The eve of May Day when witches were supposed to celebrate their Sabbath on Brocken, the highest peak in the Harz Mountains.

The world of nature

21 Nocturnal.

22 The cactus. There are 1,500 species, chiefly found in dry regions of the Tropics.

23 The bat. A highly specialized group of insectivorous mammals, with wing membranes that make them the only mammal capable of flying like birds.

24 An herbivorous animal.

25 The clock is really a cluster of feathered seeds formed from the flower. They are light enough to be blown far and wide, for the seeds to settle and ultimately grow into dandelion plants.

26 In the ridges under the crown. The crown is the wide top, like an open umbrella. The ridges are sometimes called gills. The umbrella growth is the stalk, and its

job is to scatter the cells from which the new mushrooms grow.

27 Osmosis. This is the passage of one fluid into another through a membrane between them. Osmosis takes place through a semi-permeable membrane; this allows certain substances to pass through and keeps out others.

28 Chlorophyll. Most plant cells do not produce chlorophyll/ unless the plant is exposed to sunlight.

29 1. Egg. 2. Larva or caterpillar. 3. Pupa or chrysalis/ chrysalid.

30 Cygnets . . . the young of the swan.

31 The ermine.

32 Head, thorax and abdomen.

33 The salmon. When hatched, the young are *alevins*. Once the yolk-sac is absorbed, they become *parr*, and after two years become *smolts*, when they migrate to the sea. After a year or two they return as *grilse*, and after spawning they return downstream as spent fish or *kelts*.

34 This is the way that bees can inform the other bees in a hive where nectar is to be found. A worker bee, who has been out of the hive and found a good source of nectar, 'dances' by moving in fixed patterns on the vertical honeycomb inside the hive.

35 Insects. Cochineal is obtained from the dried bodies of the females of a tropical scale insect, *Coccus cacti*. It is a scarlet or crimson dye. The insects are brushed from the cactus plants on which they live, and killed by hot water or dry heat. 70,000 insects yield only a pound of dye.

36 It has four wings. True flies have two wings.

37 Some toads have a poisonous liquid in their skin, especially in the bumps behind the eyes. It lets out this poison when it is attacked. The attacking animal can become ill or die if it touches the poison. Not all toads are venomous.

Myths and legends

38 A hammer. The Nordic god of thunder and lightning,
Thor rode the skies in his chariot. The wheels made the
rumbling of thunder; lightning flashed from his hammer,
Mjolnir, when he threw it at his enemies. Thor was also
the god of war and protector of peasants. Thursday
was named after him.

39 The goat.

40 Jason.

41 At the gate to Hades. Cerberus was a many-headed
watchdog with a voice of bronze.

42 He looked into his mirrorlike shield so that he could
see where to direct his sword to cut off her head.
Medusa and her Gorgon sisters were so ugly that anyone
who looked directly at them turned into stone. Athene
guided Perseus' hand so that he might strike the monster.

43 Nectar.

44 Hydra. It was sometimes known as Lernean Hydra
because it was supposed to live in the Lernean Marshes
in Argolis. As the second of his twelve labours, Hercules
killed the monster by burning eight of the heads and
burying the supposedly immortal one under a rock.

45 The god of sleep. The Greeks called him Hypnos, and
his three sons were Morpheus, Icelus and Phantasus.

46 The griffin. Also known as griffon, gryphon, gryphus or
gryps, it was believed by the Greeks to keep watch over
the gold of Scythia.

47 That the Greeks had beaten the Persians in the Battle
of Marathon.

48 Athena or Bellerophon. Perseus cut off the head of the
Gorgon Medusa, and the winged horse Pegasus was
born from the blood. Athena tamed Pegasus using a
golden bridle and then gave the horse to Bellerophon
who also used the golden bridle. He was finally thrown

off and Pegasus flew into the sky where Zeus made him into a constellation.

49 Zeus (king of the gods), for giving fire to man.
50 Asgard. Not Valhalla, which was a hall in Asgard where Odin held his council.
51 Helios (or Helius). Helios was god of the sun, and drove his sun chariot through the sky.
52 Leander. One night he was drowned. In anguish, Hero cast herself into the sea. The Hellespont is now called the Dardanelles.

Speed Quiz 1

53 America. The U.S. flag is also popularly known as 'Stars and Stripes' and 'Old Glory'.
54 A swan.
55 Hungary.
56 Robinson Crusoe.
57 Papyrus . . . hence *paper*.
58 Yale.
59 Australia.
60 Guinevere.
61 Lava.
62 To make it rise.
63 Shoulder blade.
64 Kingston-upon-Hull. Also Grimsby.
65 Amen.
66 Pepsin.
67 Oxford Committee for Famine Relief.
68 Tchaikovsky.
69 Rip Van Winkle.
70 180. Strictly speaking, the sum of the interior angles of a triangle is 180°.
71 Coolibah tree (Kulibar tree). From the song *Waltzing Matilda*.

72 10 . . . in addition to the three rings that consist of tiny
    particles. The tenth moon, Janus, was discovered only
    a few years ago.

Games and sport 1

73 Wrestling.
74 A strap passing under a horse's tail and fastened to the
    harness or saddle to prevent it from slipping forward.
75 A barbed hook mounted on a handle, used for landing
    fish. In fresh water, mainly for salmon and pike. At sea,
    used for fish too heavy for the landing net.
76 14.2 hands.
77 Hop, step and a jump.
78 A boxer whose stance advances the right foot and the
    right arm . . . which is opposite to that normally adopted.
79 West Germany. England won 4 – 2.
80 Glasgow Rangers.
81 Stoke City.
82 New Zealand.
83 400 metres and the 1,500 metres.
84 1. Dr. W. G. Grace. 2. Tommy Docherty.
85 1963.
86 1. Middlesex. 2. Arsenal (1950).
87 Pall-mall (pell-mell) was a game in which a ball was
    driven through an iron ring suspended in a long alley.
    The London street was once Pall-mall Alley.
88 A batsman with a stubborn defensive style. The first
    one was probably A. Jupp of Surrey who was known as
    'Young Stonewall'.
89 Iffley Road Track, Oxford on 6 May 1954.
90 Finnish. He won five gold medals at the 1924 Olympic
    Games.
91 Uruguay, Italy and Brazil.
    Uruguay 4 : Argentina 2, in Montevideo 1930

Uruguay 2 : Brazil 1, in Rio de Janeiro 1950
Italy 2 : Czechoslovakia 1, in Rome 1934
Italy 4 : Hungary 2, in Paris 1938
Brazil 5 : Sweden 2, in Stockholm 1958
Brazil 3 : Czechoslovakia 1, in Santiago 1962

Team Quiz 1

92a	His signature, or something written in his own handwriting.
92b	Some money or gift towards a cause, club, charity, etc.
93a	A rink.
93b	A range.
94a	Painting and other artistic pursuits.
94b	Knitting.
95a	The study of words.
95b	The science and study of food.
96a	The reindeer.
96b	The yak.
97a	Heathrow.
97b	Greenwich.
98a	Isle of Wight.
98b	Anglesey.
99a	Bay of Bengal.
99b	Arabian Sea.
100a	In the kitchen.
100b	In a tavern.
101a	Talk in more than one language.
101b	Use the left hand as well as the right, or able to use both hands equally well.
102a	Fagin. Both characters in *Oliver Twist* by Charles Dickens.
102b	Professor Henry Higgins. In *Pygmalion*.
103a	Egypt.
103b	Turkey.

104a Parish church of Marylebone, i.e. St Mary-le-Bone or St Mary at the Bourne.

104b Westminster Abbey.

105a St Mary-le-Bow.

105b St Clement Danes in the Strand.

106a Sir Hans Sloane in 1722.

106b Lincoln's Inn Fields.

107a Vanbrugh Castle and Blenheim Palace both designed by Sir J. Vanbrugh.

107b Marylebone Park.

Picture Quiz 1   *Famous people*

108a Mary, Queen of Scots.

b Horatio, Viscount Nelson.

c Henry VIII.

d William Shakespeare.

e Amelia Bloomer.

f Charles I.

General Knowledge 2

109 A road or street or alley that is open at one end only.

110 The size of the lens aperture. The f-number is a measure of the amount of light that a lens will allow to pass through it. Each f-number, called a stop, lets in half as much light as the next lower number. The smaller the number, the larger the aperture.

111 The appointment of the younger William Pitt at the age of 24 as Prime Minister of Britain.

112 Santiago.

113 Dick Turpin, the highwayman.

114 12. From the Latin *duodecimus* meaning twelfth.

115 15. In one hour 1/24 of 360 degrees passes beneath the Sun = 15 degrees.

116 King Edward I. Met at Westminster in 1295. Named 'Model Parliament' by 19th-century historians.

117 Mediterranean Sea.

118 *Vanity Fair*.

119 Louisa May Alcott.

120 Canberra.

121 A stone pillar – a type of monument specially characteristic of ancient Egypt. Most of them had inscriptions in hieroglyphics. They were cut at the quarry as single blocks of granite, and are upright, four-sided and narrowing to a point at the top.

122 Castor and Pollux.

123 The elastic, horny substance in the middle of the sole of a horse's foot.

124 Harold (shot in the eye at the Battle of Hastings); William Rufus (William II) – shot while hunting in the New Forest, either deliberately assassinated or killed accidentally; Richard Coeur de Lion (shot by an arrow while besieging the castle of Chaluz in France).

125 *The once and future king*. The four books are: *The*

sword in the stone, The queen of air and darkness,
The ill-made knight and *The candle in the wind.*

126 Sam Weller . . . in *Pickwick Papers* by Charles Dickens.

127 Existentialism.

Science 1

128 Carbon.

129 A crystal set is an early type of radio receiver that uses a cat's whisker and crystal combination as a detector, instead of a diode valve.

130 Sodium and chlorine. Table salt is sodium chloride. Sodium is a soft, silvery-white metal. Chlorine is a poisonous yellow-green gas.

131 Copper sulphate in acid solution, or copper cyanide in alkaline solution.

132 Einstein. E = energy, m = mass, c = velocity of light.

133 *Light Amplification by Stimulated Emission of Radiation.* A laser is a device for producing a beam of light which is: 1. Coherent (all waves in phase, a pure single sine-wave). 2. Monochromatic (one wavelength only). 3. Non-divergent (very nearly, i.e. beam hardly spreads at all over long distances). 4. Very intense. To obtain net amplification by stimulated emission, it is necessary to have an 'inverted population', i.e. more upper states than lower states.

134 Chlorine. Also added, in much smaller amounts, to drinking water.

135 The electron.

136 Gamma rays.

137 The name comes from André Marie Ampère, a Frenchman who discovered the laws of electromagnetism . . . in the 1820s. He showed that parallel electric currents attract each other if they move in the same direction, and repel if their directions are opposite. He found that

an electric current flowing through a coiled wire acts
like a magnet. His book *Theory of electrodynamic
phenomena* was published in 1826. He was a
mathematician as well as a physicist.

138   Van Allen belts of radiation. James Van Allen was an
American physicist who discovered the belts from
information collected by the *Explorer* and *Pioneer*
satellites in 1958. The belts are rings that surround the
Earth at distances that vary from a few hundred to a
few thousand miles away. They consist of electrically-
charged particles, and may one day prove a hazard to
space travel.

139   The thermal barrier occurs at the speed at which heat
created by friction reduces the strength and usefulness
of objects moving through the atmosphere. The speed
at which aircraft can travel in the air is limited by the
amount of heat their structural materials can stand.

140   An obtuse angle.

141   Nicotine. An oily, colourless, acid liquid.

142   20°. Subtract 32 and multiply by 5/9.

143   1 to 6.

Speed Quiz 2

144   U.S.S.R.

145   A hare.

146   Belgium.

147   Cuba.

148   (Lower) jaw or jaw-bone.

149   King George VI.

150   Treacle.

151   Finland.

152   Waltz (Viennese).

153   Victoria Cross.

154   Bacteria.

155 Chihuahua.

156 Atomic physicists. Some scientists believe that all the known atomic particles may be combinations of three basic bits of matter. They believe this because particles once thought to be basic break down into other particles. They decided that the basic particles have not yet been discovered.

157 A saint.

158 Libra.

159 He was a Quaker.

160 The farthing.

161 Sound.

162 Valentine's Day. The feast day of the Roman martyr St Valentine of the 4th century AD.

163 Town or city hall.

Quotations 1

164 Napoleon I (1769–1821).

165 *The Rubá'iyát of Omar Khayyám* translated by Edward Fitzgerald.

166 Mr Micawber, in *David Copperfield* by Charles Dickens.

167 Charles II (1630–1685).

168 Phineas T. Barnum (1810–1891).

169 *Peter Pan* by J. M. Barrie.

170 Hermann Goering.

171 Lewis Carroll (real name Charles Lutwidge Dodgson). The quotation is from *Alice in Wonderland.*

172 Julius Caesar, at the crossing of the Rubicon.

173 Winnie-the-Pooh, in the book of the same name by A. A. Milne.

174 Sir Winston Churchill, on 13 May 1940 during the Second World War.

175 Benjamin Franklin (1706–1790).

General Knowledge 3

176 Beatrix Potter.

177 Buonaparte (or Bonaparte).

178 The grooved piece of iron at the place in a railway where tracks cross. It enables the wheels of a train running on one track to cross the rail of another track.

179 The occurrence of earthquake shocks.

180 Hurricanes. The American Weather Bureau uses a permanent list of about 80 girls' names to label each season's hurricanes.

181 He was playing bowls on Plymouth Hoe. 'There is time enough to finish the game and beat the Spaniards too.'

182 Israel.

183 Red, varying from crimson to brilliant orange.

184 (Spanish-Portugal) Iberian Peninsula.

185 Because he could expect to receive postcards from you ... and a deltiologist is a collector of postcards.

186 Norwegian. During the second World War, Vidkun Quisling aided the Germans in their invasion of Norway and was made puppet prime minister. He fled at the defeat of Germany, and was executed on 24 October 1945. 'Quisling' is now a term applied to a traitor and collaborationist in time of enemy occupation.

187 The Pope. He receives it when he is crowned. It bears his name and the picture of St Peter in a boat. All papal documents must be stamped with this signet. When the Pope dies, the ring is broken.

188 Boldwood shot and killed her husband Sergeant Troy, and was sentenced to imprisonment.

189 He suffers from colour blindness. It is used especially when a person can only differentiate between two of the three primary colours.

190 Salic Law. It was a form of Salic Law that prevented Queen Victoria from succeeding the kingdom of Hanover.

191 He introduced the Beaufort Scale, a table to describe
the force of winds. The table is based on the effects of
winds on sailing ships. Beaufort was born in Navan in
Meath, Ireland, in 1774. He was an hydrographer to
the Navy from 1822–1855.

192 Doge.

193 The broad strait that separates Lewis Island in the
Hebrides from the north-west coast of Scotland.

Team Quiz 2

194a 31.

194b 29.

195a 10.

195b 100 years old.

196a A small airfield or pad where helicopters land, e.g.
Battersea Heliport in London.

196b A yacht with wheels that 'sails' along the sandy shore.
Sand yacht racing is now popular in many parts of the
world.

197a He studies the motions and phenomena of atmosphere,
especially for weather forecasting.

197b He explores or studies caves.

198a The Vatican, Rome.

198b Versailles. The former royal palace, near Paris.

199a 2. From 'bi' meaning 'two'.

199b 6. All mature insects have 6 legs. An immature larval
form of an insect may appear to have more than 6 legs,
e.g. most caterpillars.

200a Vitamin C.

200b Vitamin D.

201a Silver. The symbol is short for the Latin name for
silver, *argentum*.

201b Copper. The symbol is short for the Latin name for
copper, *cuprum*.

202a By knocking its head as it bores through wood.

202b By rubbing its forewings together.

203a Reredos.

203b Purdah.

204a Rugby.

204b Greyfriars School.

205a It must be held not later than five years after the previous election.

205b Four years. But a President can be re-elected for one additional term of office.

206a King Alexander III. The Norwegian fleet was routed by heavy storms, enabling the Scots to win the Battle of Largs. King Hahon of Norway died and his successor Magnus IV ceded the Western Isles and the Isle of Man to Scotland by the Treaty of Perth 1266.

206b Alba. Kenneth MacAlpin, King of the Scots, claimed the throne of the Picts in about 844, and established Alba, which was the first united Kingdom in Scotland.

207a Wallace won the Battle of Stirling Bridge against Edward I of England, 1297. He was defeated at Falkirk in 1298.

207b Her father was King Eric II of Norway, her mother was Queen Margaret of Norway. On the death of her maternal grandfather, Alexander III of Scotland, the Maid became Queen of Scotland and was betrothed to Edward, son of Edward I of England. But she died during her passage to Scotland.

208a James II was beseiging Roxburgh Castle, held by the English. He was killed when a cannon exploded.

208b James I of Scotland.

209a 'Rob Roy' is Gaelic for 'Red Robert', and he was called by this name because of his red hair. Rob Roy was born Robert MacGregor but later took the surname Campbell.

209b The name 'Stuart' is derived from 'steward'. Ancestors of the last Stuart king held the office of High Stewards of Scotland.

Picture Quiz 2   *Ships and Boats*

210 (i) Sir Francis Chichester.
(ii) Gypsy Moth IV.

211 Coracle.

212 Chinese junk.

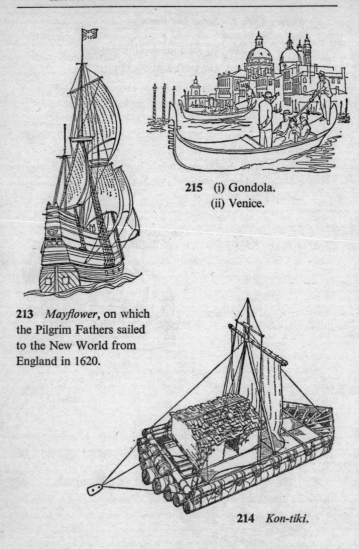

215 (i) Gondola.
(ii) Venice.

213 *Mayflower*, on which the Pilgrim Fathers sailed to the New World from England in 1620.

214 *Kon-tiki.*

The Bible

216 Book. From the Greek *biblion*. The word *biblion* itself came from *biblos* meaning 'papyrus' or 'paper'.

217 Eat of the forbidden fruit. From Genesis 2 and 3.

218 He kissed him so that the soldiers could identify him and arrest him. From Matthew 26: 47–50.

219 14. Originally Jacob had to serve 7 years, but was then 'tricked' by his father-in-law Laban who gave him his elder daughter Leah after the 7 years. He later married Rachel, but had to serve Laban another 7 years. From Genesis 29: 15–30.

220 6. From Genesis 1 and 2.

221 12. From Genesis 35: 22.

222 Joseph of Arimathea. From Matthew 27: 57–60.

223 Barabbas. From Mark 15: 15.

224 Bethlehem.

225 Golgotha or Calvary.

226 Delilah found that his strength lay in his hair, and had his head shaved as he slept.

227 Jonathan.

228 Benjamin.

229 Abednego and Meshach.

230 Cain.

231 Simon.

232 River Jordan.

233 The head of John the Baptist. She is not named in the gospels, but is traditionally called Salome. Herod promised her the reward.

234 John Wycliffe. This first translation of the Bible into English was published in 1388. The peasants' revolt in 1381 had convinced Wycliffe of the necessity to appeal directly to the masses.

General Knowledge 4

235 Jupiter.

236 Turkey. About 4 miles from the Hellespont. The ruins were revealed in the 1870s, by Heinrich Schliemann.

237 60.

238 To attract the birds and insects in order to pollinate the flower. Pollination is the transfer of pollen to fertilize a flower from the anther of one plant to the stigma of another.

239 Buns.

240 Saladin. He brought about the Third Crusade by capturing Jerusalem in 1187. He made a truce with Richard I in 1192.

241 The tank. When the machines were being built, officers called them 'water tanks', 'cisterns', 'reservoirs' to keep the secret, and the name 'tank' stuck. The tank is a motor-driven combat vehicle enclosed in armour plate mounted on caterpillar tracks. The Somme Offensive took place in 1916.

242 California.

243 A Christian chorister . . . by Jews.

244 Magog. Their effigies have stood in the Guildhall since the 15th century. Twice replaced: after the Great Fire of 1666 and after an air raid in 1940.

245 Machiavelli. We talk of 'machiavellian cunning'. Nicolo Machiavelli was born in 1469. The great source of his reputation is his book *The Prince*, published in 1532. He believed that all means may be resorted to to maintain authority, and that all treacherous acts of a ruler are justified by the wickedness of the governed.

246 Buffalo or deer meat, dried meat, venison, bison . . . dried and pounded into powder, and mixed with hot fat. Cooled and cut into cakes. Berries might be added to give a flavour. North American Indians first made it.

247 Lockjaw.

248 Black.

249 Konrad Adenauer.

History miscellany 1

250 Druids. They lived in Gaul and Britain, and worshipped ancient gods similar to those of the Greek and Roman.

251 The public square or market-place, where people assembled to discuss politics or business.

252 The money paid by the king to the Danes to bribe them to leave Britain.

253 King Richard III, who was killed in the battle.

254 To kidnap men to serve in the Navy.

255 Oliver Cromwell.

256 He was a Portuguese prince who planned expeditions and worked to perfect navigational instruments, although he never went on any long voyage himself. He settled near Cape Saint Vincent in south-west Portugal in the 15th century, and surrounded himself with scholars, map-makers and sea captains.

257 They were farm workers of Dorset who were transported to a penal colony for organizing a Trades Union.

258 They were 'poor priests' not all of whom were members of the clergy. John Wycliffe, who made a systematic translation of the Bible into English, instructed them and sent them out on foot to spread the message of the Bible. They were greatly persecuted.

259 During the war with revolutionary France, French frigates landed about 1,400 soldiers ashore in Fishguard Bay. They surrendered to the local militia almost without striking a blow.

260 United States, Russia and the United Kingdom.

261 Tigris and Euphrates.

262 Thomas Cromwell negotiated the marriage of King Henry VIII to Anne of Cleves. The king took an instant dislike to her, calling her the 'Flanders Mare'. Cromwell was in disgrace, and although he helped to dissolve the marriage, he was beheaded on Tower Hill.

263 The Court of Star Chamber. It dealt with offenders who were too powerful for the ordinary law courts. The ceiling of the room where the Court met was decorated with stars.

264 On the block or the gallows. In 1536, people in Lincolnshire and Yorkshire were disturbed by three commissions which they felt might lead to the suppression of parish churches. Insurrections broke out, and about 200 rebels were executed.

265 Crimean War. The treaty was signed by Russia, France, Great Britain, Turkey and Sardinia.

266 Senlac Hill. The scene of the Battle of Hastings, sometimes called the Battle of Senlac.

Team Quiz 3

267a Eskimos. Many still do.
267b American (or Red) Indians.
268a Paris.
268b Moscow.
269a China.
269b India.
270a The eagle. Usually built on rocky crags or tree tops. They often return to the same eyrie each year and build on to the old nest.
270b The squirrel. Built in trees, of sticks and moss.
271a Cardiff.
271b Sunderland.
272a River Danube ... to the Black Sea. Otherwise Austria is landlocked.

272b   The Rhine, which rises in eastern Switzerland.

273a   A headland in Dorset on the south coast of England.

273b   A harbour or sea basin. A famous naval anchorage surrounded by the Orkney Islands off the northern coast of Scotland.

274a   Roaring Forties.

274b   Doldrums.

275a   The cuckoo.

275b   The grouse.

276a   Beggars must take what is given to them, and not dictate what they like best.

276b   Because if you venture everything on one speculation or idea, if it fails everything will be lost.

277a   Celsius. Developed by Anders Celsius in 1742 who originally had the centigrade scale the other way round – the freezing point of water was 100° and the boiling point 0°. The scale was inverted a year or two later.

277b   Aneroid barometer.

278a   De Medici.

278b   Sitwell.

279a   Stockton and Darlington Railway, in 1825.

279b   The Rocket, Novelty, Sans Pareil, Perseverance.

280a   William Huskisson. The accident, commemorated by a monument at Newton-le-Willows, happened not very far from Lymm.

280b   George Stephenson 1781–1848.

281a   London and York. An extension of Ermine Street runs northwards from York to the Wall of Antoninus in Scotland.

281b   A2 = Dover road; A3 = Portsmouth road; A5 = Holyhead road.

282a   'Blind Jack' Metcalf of Knaresborough. He lost his eyesight at 6, and from 1765 constructed 185 miles of road and numerous bridges.

282b   Thomas Telford.

Music and song

283 Opera. Latin *opus* = work. The plural is *opera*.

284 Mezzo-soprano.

285 Baritone.

286 A small keyboard instrument of the harpsichord family, in which the strings are plucked when the keys are depressed. It has an oblong box-shaped body, and was common in the 16th and 17th centuries.

287 A complete set of pipes of the same tone, one or more pipes for each note. They are controlled by stop knobs on the organ console.

288 He was a gold-miner . . . in the Californian gold rush of 1849.

289 Piano.

290 Yehudi Menuhin – violin. Jacqueline du Pré – 'cello.

291 A cradle song or lullaby. Usually an instrumental piece suggestive of a cradle song, although it has no words.

292 1. Sir Henry Wood (1869–1944). 2. Queen's Hall, London.

293 Metal strings, strung over a shallow closed box, are struck with two hammers.

294 An instrumental composition with three or four movements with contrasts in both tempo and key. Designed chiefly for solo instruments or one or two instruments.

295 Songs. A *Lied* is simply a song with German words, but in other languages the word is used for the special type of German song associated particularly with the names of Schubert, Schumann, Brahms and Hugo Wolf.

296 Prima donna.

297 Psalm 98. 'O sing unto the Lord a new song; For He hath done marvellous things . . .' Latin *cantate* = sing ye.

298 The steady swelling and decreasing of vocal volume in one long held note.

299 Named from the Italian town of Taranto, habitat of
the tarantula spider. Superstition declared the tarantula
poisonous, and the dance was said to be the result of
(sometimes the cure for) this poison.

300 (John Philip) Sousa. E.g. 'The Washington Post',
'Stars and Stripes Forever'.

Who am I?

301 George Whitefield. He was a great English evangelist
and one of the founders of Methodism.

302 Sir John Douglas Cockcroft. He died in September 1967.

303 Rodney George (Rod) Laver.

304 Alexander Dubcek.

305 Axel Martin Fredrik Munthe.

306 Earl Russell, Bertrand Arthur William. He died on
2 February 1970.

307 Willy Brandt.

308 Boris Leonidovich Pasternak.

309 Sir William Henry Bragg.

310 Vicente Blasco Ibanez.

311 General Franco.

312 Mrs Ann Jones, formerly Ann Haydon.

313 Wilfred Owen.

314 Martin Luther King, Jr.

315 Pierre Elliott Trudeau.

316 Bertolt Brecht.

Speed Quiz 3

317 Sweden.

318 The Pekingese.

319 The sun. From Latin *parare* = to ward; *sol* = sun, via
Italian.

320 Fauna.

321 Blackberries.

322 Diameter.

323 Sorbonne.

324 Job.

325 The Muezzin. He climbs a mosque tower, called a minaret, to do so five times a day.

326 Mr Rochester.

327 Polonius.

328 Red.

329 A breed of dog . . . Kerry Blue Terrier, so called because it was originally bred in County Kerry in Ireland and has a soft, short, blue-grey coat.

330 90 degrees.

331 Mercury.

332 Columbine. Stock characters in the Italian comedies of the 16th and 17th centuries, from which our pantomime is derived.

333 A German submarine. First used in World War I, the phrase stands for *Unterseeboot* (undersea boat).

334 Wales. It is the Welsh for 'Wales'.

335 Aristotle. His full name is Aristotle Socrates Onassis; Socrates was another Greek philosopher.

336 In lilac time.

337 The roots. The plant is a herb, and the roots are long and sweet-tasting. The plant grows mainly in southern Europe, but also to a lesser degree in Asia. The tap-root is sliced and boiled. As the extracted juice solidifies, it is made into black sticks.

Shakespeare

338 1. *The Tempest*. 2. Ariel.

339 Puck.

340 Pease Blossom, Cobweb, Moth and Mustard Seed.

341 Prospero.

342 1. Lady Macbeth. 2. The king – Duncan.
343 Claudius (the King of Denmark).
344 Malcolm.
345 1. 3,000 ducats. 2. Three months.
346 Romeo Montague and Juliet Capulet.
347 A seaport in Cyprus.
348 Montano.
349 Claudius.
350 Touchstone.
351 Tennis balls . . . in lieu of certain dukedoms claimed by the English king.
352 She is bitten by a snake (asp) which she applies to her breast.
353 Portia.
354 Puck . . . in *A Midsummer Night's Dream.*
355 Hermione, the queen, was alive although Leontes, her husband, thought she was dead. She is shown to him as a statue, and comes alive when he expresses his sorrow and love for her.

Picture Quiz 3 Buildings

356 Glamis Castle, in Scotland.

357 (i) The Globe, Southwark.
     (ii) William Shakespeare.

358 (i) Sir Christopher Wren. (ii) St Paul's, London.

359 Hatfield House, in Hertfordshire.

360 Silkweaving. The workrooms were on the top floor.

361 Treetops Hotel, Kenya, for the observation of wildlife.

General Knowledge 5

362 First Lord of the Treasury.

363 Boadicea.

364 Pluto.

365 Tunisia.

366 They use these sounds, which are too high for us to hear, to help them navigate in the dark. The sound waves strike objects in the path of flight and send back echoes to the bats' ears. The echoes tell the bats how to turn so that they can avoid the obstacles.

367 Maid Marian. She does not belong to the original cycle of ballads, but is the afterthought of a later age.

368 Wales. It refers to all the mountain regions in Wales. 'Cambria' is the old word meaning 'Wales'.

369 Land or fields. 1 rood = $\frac{1}{4}$ acre.

370 Psalms.

371 A sphere.

372 He cut through it with his sword. The Gordian Knot was used by a Phrygian peasant to tie the ox yoke to his chariot. He became King of Phrygia. A legend said that whoever loosened the Gordian Knot would rule all Asia. Alexander the Great cut it with his sword (334 BC) and marched on to conquest.

   Cutting the Gordian Knot = solving a difficult problem in an unexpected way, *or* disposing of a difficulty by bold measures, or summarily.

373 St Columba.

374 The Althing. It is the oldest European parliamentary body in existence, dating from 930 AD.

375 Sinn Fein. It played a big part in achieving independence for the Republic of Ireland.

376 Utopia. The book *Utopia* was published by Sir Thomas More in Latin in 1516 and was translated into English in 1551. The story is based on the imaginary report of

Ralph Hythlodaye, whom More describes as a Portuguese sailor who had made three voyages with Amerigo Vespucci.

377 They met on a raft anchored in the Neman River. On 14 June 1807, Napoleon routed the Russian armies at Friedland, and forced Czar Alexander I to seek peace. The peace was signed in Tilsit, and the preliminaries were settled by the emperors on the raft.

378 A heart transplant – the first human heart transplant in medical history. The hospital is in Cape Town. A 30-man surgical team performed the operation, headed by Dr Christiaan Neethling Barnard. The heart was removed from a 25-year-old woman who had died in a motor-car accident, and placed in the chest of 55-year-old Louis Washkansky. He died of a lung infection 18 days later. The second transplant on Philip Blaiberg on 2 January 1968 was more successful.

Team Quiz 4

379a Tea.

379b Golf clubs.

380a A kind of tree. Monkeys find it difficult to climb. Correct name is Chilean Pine.

380b A breed of dog.

381a Spelling the word as it sounded.

381b Copying out the notes word for word.

382a They have teeth especially adapted for gnawing.

382b It is capable of grasping like a hand.

383a It does not possess a tail.

383b It has very short legs. Name comes from German; *Dachs* = badger, *Hund* = dog.

384a French. Born in Brittany.

384b Italian. Born on the island of Sicily.

385a   Prince Arthur. Henry's elder brother, who died in 1502. The wife was Catherine of Aragon.

385b   Marie Louise. Archduchess, daughter of Emperor Francis I of Austria, II of the Holy Roman Empire.

386a   Einstein. Albert Einstein introduced the theory in two parts: the special theory dealing with electrodynamics and optics in 1905, and the general theory on gravity c. 1916.

386b   (Sir Isaac) Newton. The alleged fall of an apple that started Newton thinking about gravity took place in 1665; his book *Philosophae Naturalis Principia Mathematica* expounding the theory was published in 1687.

387a   Mr Toad. In Kenneth Grahame's *The wind in the willows*.

387b   D'Artagnan. In Alexander Dumas' *The three musketeers*.

388a   Eeyore, the old grey donkey.

388b   Wackford Squeers.

389a   The owl and the pussycat.

389b   The Jumblies.

390a   Christian. In John Bunyan's *The pilgrim's progress*.

390b   Gulliver. In *Gulliver's travels* by Jonathan Swift.

391a   David Lloyd-George, 1863–1945.

391b   Aneurin Bevan, 1897–1960.

392a   Lake Bala in Merionethshire.

392b   River Towy. It rises in the Cambrian Mountains and flows into Carmarthen Bay. 65 miles long.

393a   Emlyn Williams, born 1905 in Flintshire.

393b   Richard Llewellyn, born 1907.

394a   Robert Stephenson, son of George Stephenson who built many railway bridges and viaducts.

394b   Ivor Novello.

Games and sport 2

395   The goalkeeper.

396   The end of the race.

397 Fencing ... it signifies a 'touch' or a score.

398 Boxing. Compiled by the Marquis of Queensberry and Arthur Chambers in 1867.

399 On a bobsleigh or toboggan. Cresta is an artificial run at St Moritz in Switzerland.

400 Billiards or snooker. They are the long tapering rods with leather and fibre tips that are used to strike the ball. 'Cue' is also a term used in acting.

401 Basketball.

402 1. In Scotland. 2. Hockey. It is very much like the Irish game of hurling.

403 1. Cricket. 2. England and Australia.

404 Canada.

405 1. 8 in Australia. 2. 6 in England. The rules provide for either 6 or 8 'according to the agreed conditions of play'.

406 The crawl.

407 14.

408 The pommel is the part of a saddle that sticks up at the front.

409 In polo. Usually lasts $7\frac{1}{2}$ minutes. From the Hindustani *chakar* meaning wheels. Alternative spellings: chukkar, chukka, chucker.

410 A trophy awarded by the former American President for competition by national amateur teams of golfers.

411 20.

412 Stones.

413 When he 'castles' – he moves the castle and the king at the same time.

414 20. Each boxer starts a round with a maximum of 20, from which a number may be subtracted. The man with the higher number wins the round. If both are level at the end, one extra mark can be awarded to one of the boxers.

Poets and poetry

415 John Milton.

416 Robert Browning.

417 'Nor any drop to drink' or 'And all the boards did shrink'. By Samuel Taylor Coleridge.

418 '. . . and gimble in the wabe'. From *Through the looking glass* by Lewis Carroll.

419 *King Lear*, Act III Scene IV.

420 *The Rubá'iyát of Omar Khayyám*.

421 'Sohrab and Rustum'.

422 'Tam O'Shanter' by Robert Burns. The quotation is from Gavin Douglas.

423 *Morte d'Arthur*.

424 Queen Victoria. Beginning, "Ave ye 'eard o' the Widow at Windsor, With a hairy gold crown on her 'ead?"

425 'Kubla Khan', written by Samuel Taylor Coleridge in 1797 when he was staying in south-west England.

426 John Keats, in a sonnet. He died at the age of 26.

Master brain 1

427 It is added to petrol to prevent 'knocking', and is known as 'anti-knock'.

428 Sir Christopher Wren.

429 An assize in which there is no person to be brought to trial. Formerly an assize at which no prisoner was condemned to death.

430 The nadir.

431 Sir Winston Churchill.

432 Parallax. It becomes more noticeable with close-up pictures, and results from the fact that the camera lens and the viewfinder lens 'look' at views from slightly different angles.

433 Boyle's Law, Charles' Law and Avogadro's Law. Written: $PV = nRT$.

434 Sir William Smith . . . in Glasgow.

435 Napoleon gave himself up to the British after his defeat at Waterloo. After Waterloo, he abdicated a second time. Fouché, the French president, ordered him to leave Paris. The Prussians were after his blood, and the British cruisers at Rochefort cut off his possible escape to the United States. Napoleon then appealed to the British government for protection in a letter to the Prince Regent in which he compared himself to Themistocles. Napoleon boarded the *Bellerophon* on 15 July, and was taken to Plymouth. From there he was taken to St Helena.

Themistocles was an Athenian statesman and soldier in the Persian Wars of about 500 BC. He destroyed the Persian fleet at Salamis. Despite all he had done for them, the Athenians banished him in about 471 BC. He then went to Persia where he was warmly welcomed and given an estate in Magnesia, where he stayed until his death.

436 It is one of the nine isotopes of plutonium. It is the most important because it is fissionable. Pu-239 is manufactured in quantities in uranium chain reactors by bombarding uranium with neutrons. It serves as a source of energy in nuclear explosions and nuclear reactors.

437 The Venerable Bede.

438 Trinculo.

439 In early years the railways were mainly built to the standard gauge of 4 ft. 8½ inches. Isambard Kingdom Brunel of the Great Western Railway introduced a broad gauge of 7 ft. 0¼ inches. There were a number of variations and quarrels until the 'narrow gauge' won by legislation in 1846.

440 The speed of rotation of a spinning shaft or wheel. Usually measured in terms of revolution per minute (rpm). A speedometer, by measuring the rotation of wheels, is a form of tachometer.

441 One. One squared = one. Cube of one = one.

442 Samuel Richardson (the book was *Pamela*).

General Knowledge 6

443 The coronation of Queen Elizabeth II.

444 A ghostly or spiritual one that is supposed to make its presence known by tappings, slamming of doors and other remarkable inexplicable happenings. A main attribute of a poltergeist is that it is supposed to throw things about. The name comes from German, and means 'noisy ghost'.

445 Calcium carbonate.

446 A small board supported on two castors and a pencil. When the fingers rest lightly on the board, the pencil is supposed to write words, sentences and messages under a spiritual influence.

447 *On the origin of species by means of natural selection.* Written by Charles Darwin and first published in 1859, the book is generally known as *Origin of species*.

448 Belgium . . . because it has been the site of more European battles than any other country.

449 Giuseppe Garibaldi's thousand volunteers who fought for the unity of Italy in 1860. They wore red shirts as a uniform.

450 King Henry VIII. The title was conferred by Pope Leo X in 1521 and confirmed by Parliament in 1544. All subsequent British monarchs have borne this title.

451 The litre.

452 Kemal Ataturk. He founded the Republic of Turkey, and was President from 1923 until his death in 1938.

453 The famous horse of King Richard II which ate from his hand.

454 Balaclava, in the Crimean War.

455 A Post Office department where letters are kept until called for.

456 Charlotte, Emily and Anne. The rector was Patrick Bronte; he had two other daughters who died in childhood.

457 The Salvation Army. General Booth's paper first appeared on 29 December 1879. He also founded *Christian Mission Magazine* (1870) and *The East London Evangelist* (1868).

458 A vast sea monster living at the bottom of the sea. It destroyed ships and humans. Appears in *The kraken wakes* by John Wyndham.

Picture Quiz 4   History

459 (i) Sphinx. (ii) Egypt.

460 They are Victorian bathing machines, found at the seaside. They were used to carry people out into deeper water, and for changing in.

461 Jousting.

462 A woman is being ducked in a ducking-stool, as a punishment for some misdemeanour.

463 Beating hemp.

464 They are using a hand-mill to grind corn.

Team Quiz 5

465a Alfred the Great.

465b Canute.

466a Louis Braille.

466b Marconi.

467a Flock together.

467b Two in the bush.

468a Nucleus.

468b Electrons.

469a Saint Matthew.

469b Saint Paul.

470a A general term that applies to Oxford and Cambridge Universities jointly.

470b A fictional village where the radio family of the Archers and their friends are supposed to live.

471a Mississippi.

471b Rhine.

472a Vulcan. Vulcanizing rubber is to treat rubber with sulphur or a sulphur compound and subject it to heat.

472b Morpheus.

473a The mosquito.

473b The flea. Carried in the fur of rats.

474a Sir John Hunt.

474b Frank Borman.

475a Cells (the structure of cells).

475b Stuffs and mounts the skins of animals.

476a Francis Durbridge.

476b Leslie Charteris.

477a There was a cathedral originally at Old Sarum. For various reasons the see was transferred to New Sarum. This became New Saresbury, and finally Salisbury.

477b During the Christmas season, a choir boy was elected to act as bishop. The custom was suppressed by Henry VIII, revived by Mary, and suppressed again by Queen Elizabeth I.

478a Wessex.

478b Melchester Cathedral.

479a Prince Richard and King William II (William Rufus).

479b They were the judicial officers responsible for enforcing the law in the royal forests and directing their maintenance. The 'Verderers' Hall is in King's House at Lyndhurst.

480a He was killed by a stag when he was hunting. He had not yet reached the age of knighthood.

480b He was killed by an arrow from an unknown hand, on 2 August 1100. William Tirel was the main suspect. He was close at hand, and fled the country afterwards.

Literature

481 A mouse. The lion had shown mercy to him previously. In return, the mouse nibbled through the ropes that held the lion and set him free.

482 Uncle Remus. Narrator of a cycle of stories in Joel Chandler Harris's collection of southern Negro folk tales.

483 David Copperfield. His first wife is Dora Spenlow, daughter of Mr Spenlow.

484 John Galsworthy.

485 Black Beauty, in the novel of that name by Anna Sewell.

486 Daphne du Maurier. Gerald du Maurier (1873–1934) acted in *Trilby*.

487 Percy Bysshe Shelley. Mary Wollstonecraft Shelley was his second wife, and *Frankenstein*, her first and most impressive novel, appeared in 1818.

488 Chauvelin. He became a revolutionary with a fanatical anxiety to trap Sir Percy Blakeney, the Scarlet Pimpernel, in Baroness Orczy's book.

489 Through a wardrobe. In *The lion, the witch and the wardrobe* by C. S. Lewis.

490 George Orwell.

491 Joseph Conrad (1857–1924) became a naturalized Briton in 1886. Among his famous novels of the sea are *An outcast of the islands, Lord Jim, Nostromo, Under western eyes*.

492 Magwitch, the convict.

493 Sir Thomas Malory. This English writer who died in 1471 collected the stories from French Arthurian tales and then rewrote them. It was the first important English prose romance, and was published by Caxton in 1485. Believed to be a Warwickshire knight, Malory served in the Parliament of 1445, but was arrested and convicted several times for robbery and assault. Most of his work was written in prison, and he calls himself the 'knyht presoner'.

494 *Troilus and Criseyde*. (Shakespeare's play is *Troilus and Cressida*).

495 *The power and the glory.*

496 Sancho Panza . . . in *Don Quixote of La Mancha* by Cervantes.

General Knowledge 7

497 Salmon return generally to the same river in which they were born when they are ready to spawn and die. This homing instinct encourages them to overcome obstacles. They leap through rapids and up waterfalls. These runs may take several months. Many salmon are killed. In some instances salmon ladders which consist of sloping steps help them. Those which finally get 'home' spawn and die.

498 French.

499 St Joan of Arc.

500 A cone.

501 Kindergarten. The name was originally coined by Friedrich Froebel, the German educationist, more than 100 years ago.

502 Tears. The lachrymal glands lie under the outer part of the upper eyelid. Two small tubes, the lachrymal ducts, open at the inner corner of each eyelid. They continually drain the tears from the eye to the nose.

503 Snow White.

504 Norway or Denmark. Sweden has the *krona*.

505 Dr Blimber. Paul Dombey in *Dombey and Son* was a pupil in Blimber Academy.

506 Moths and butterflies.

507 The Quakers, or Society of Friends. They originally called themselves Children of the Light, Friends or

Friends in Truth. The name Quakers was given to the Society in 1650 by Justice Bennett.

508 These ten days were omitted when Pope Gregory XIII reformed the calendar.

509 Edward Gibbon 1737–1794.

510 *Early Bird*. Three experimental satellites preceded *Early Bird* (*Telstar*, *Relay* and *Syncom*), but they were not commercially viable although they transmitted television programmes. There were also 'passive' balloon satellites such as *Echo*.

511 Adolf Hitler. He was serving a prison sentence at the time. In 1923 he had tried to overthrow the Bavarian government in the 'Beer Hall Putsch'. The plot failed. Hitler was arrested and sentenced to five years in prison for treason. He served only nine months of the sentence. Ultimately he became the *Führer* of Germany and led the country into World War II.

512 River Weser.

513 A tiger.

Science 2

514 Nitrogen. Ammonia = nitrogen and hydrogen; Laughing gas = nitrous oxide; Dynamite contains nitroglycerin.

515 Heavy water (Deuterium oxide, D_2O).

516 Solid carbon dioxide, CO_2, used as a refrigerant because it passes directly from the solid state to the gaseous state at $-78 \cdot 5°C$ at normal atmospheric pressure, with the absorption of a great deal of heat.

517 Iron pyrites (FeS_2) or Copper pyrites ($CuFeS_2$). 'Pyrites' is a common term for either. Often mistaken by early prospectors for gold ore, it can sometimes be seen in a lump of coal.

518 Nitrogen. (Nitrogen 78·09%, Oxygen 20·95%, Argon 0·93%, Others 0·03%).

519 7. The number indicates the concentration of hydrogen ions in a solution.

520 14·7. The pressure decreases with altitude because of less air pressing from above.

521 Magnesium.

522 Uranium.

523 Deoxyribonucleic Acid. DNA plays a vital part in heredity.

524 Paramecium. Any ciliated freshwater protozoan of the genus *Paramecium* having an oval body and a long, deep, oval groove.

525 Perihelion.

526 Boyle's. Pressure multiplied by volume remains constant at constant temperature.

527 The series of two-men space-flights which gave United States astronauts practice in making many vital manoeuvres they had to perform before travelling to the Moon and exploring space. Important manoeuvres were: White's space walk, rendezvous in space of *Gemini* 6 and 7, docking two space-craft.

528 Ammonia . . . from nitrogen and hydrogen. One part of nitrogen unites with three parts of hydrogen. The reaction takes place at 550°C.

529 Sodium sulphate.

530 The movement of the planets. 1. Every planet follows an elliptic orbit round the Sun. 2. Planets move faster when they are closer to the Sun. 3. The time taken for a planet to make a complete trip around the Sun is its period. The squares of the periods of two planets are proportional to the cubes of their mean distances from the Sun.

531 Henri Becquerel. He shared the Nobel Prize for physics with the Curies in 1903.

532 Joule. Named after the British scientist James P. Joule. The use of one joule in one second is equal to one watt.

Quotations 2

533 John Bunyan . . . *The Pilgrim's Progress.*

534 (i) The Coronation Service. (ii) The Holy Bible.

535 'And hand in hand, on the edge of the sand,
They danced by the light of the moon.'
From 'The owl and the pussy-cat' by Edward Lear.

536 Karl Marx (1818–1883) in the introduction to *Kritik der Hegelschen Rechtsphilosophie.*

537 Mary Tudor (1516–1558).

538 John Keats (1795–1821), from 'To Autumn'.

539 Johann Wolfgang von Goethe (1749–1832).

540 Walter de la Mare, in 'Silver'.

541 Thomas Alva Edison (1847–1931).

542 Aunt Ada Doom in *Cold Comfort Farm* by Stella Gibbons.

543 Robert Frost.

544 Rev. William Archibald Spooner. Such transpositions of initial sounds of spoken words have become known as Spoonerisms.

545 J. Alfred Prufrock, from 'The love song of J. Alfred Prufrock' by T. S. Eliot.

General Knowledge 8

546 He was the god of the Sun. Re (or Ra) was represented either in human form or with the head of a falcon and a human body. The sun disc was his symbol. He was worshipped mainly at Heliopolis, the sun city. Osiris was god of the dead, Re (pronounced 'Ray') was god of the living. The pharaohs considered themselves sons of Re.

547 Lamas. The traditional head of the Lamas is the Dalai Lama who now lives in India.

548 Henry Ford.

549 Galileo.

550 1. Archeozoic. 2. Proterozoic.

551 To string Ulysses' great bow. Penelope was the wife of Ulysses (Odysseus) and thought she was his widow when he failed to return from Troy. Each suitor, given the test, failed to accomplish it until a beggar succeeded. He turned out to be Ulysses in disguise.

552 Mammoth. Could be 11 to 12 feet high, and tusks could be 13 feet long. Lived during the Ice Age, and bodies have been discovered preserved in the ice in Siberia.

553 They contained the pumps from which medicinal water was dispensed.

554 Arthur Miller.

555 The sperm whale. It is the waxy substance obtained from the head of the sperm whale. Some spermaceti is obtained from the bottle-nosed and giant bottle-nosed whales.

556 Beads made from shells. They are white and purple or black beads used for money or ceremonial gifts or ornaments.

557 River Missouri.

558 Agoraphobia.

559 House of Keys.

560 Kibbutz (singular). Kibbutzim (plural). There are various forms of collectives in Israel including the *Moshav Ovdim* (or workers' settlement) and the *Moshav Shitufi* (or co-operative corporation farm).

561 Black Sea and Caspian Sea. The Caucasus Mountains are in Russia, and the highest peak is Elbruz (about 18,470 feet).

562 Deep blue.

563 About 25,000 miles. It is actually 24,901 miles at ground level at the equator; just over 100 miles shorter round the poles.

564 1. Prince Arthur (elder brother of Henry, who died at the age of 16). 2. Henry (who became Henry VIII).

History miscellany 2

565 Picts (and Scots).

566 The royal council of wisemen who helped the king to rule.

567 The Black Prince. Prince Edward was aged 16 when he gained the rank of knighthood at the Battle of Crecy in 1346.

568 Abraham Lincoln.

569 Nelson clapped his telescope to his blind eye and studied the signal. 'I really do not see the signal,' he said to an aide. He ignored the order and turned possible defeat into a great victory.

570 Franklin D. Roosevelt.

571 Mediterranean Sea. The two nations were Rome and Carthage (in northern Africa).

572 Crown Prince Alexis, the eldest son of Czar Nicholas II, suffered from a rare blood disease, haemophilia. Rasputin, a Siberian peasant who was a holy man in a religious sect, was introduced to Court in 1907 because he claimed to have healing powers, and indeed did seem to be successful in his treatment of the boy. However, he extended his influence, and interfered in political affairs. He was assassinated in 1916.

573 The Khedive of Egypt was forced to offer the stock (nearly half) for sale to meet his debts. Disraeli heard of this and bought the shares on behalf of Britain.

574 David Rizzio. He was stabbed to death by Darnley, the queen's husband, in March 1566.

575 Duke of Wellington.

576 Nicholas II.

577 Karl Marx.

578 Napoleon, called the 'Little Corporal' because of his small stature (about 5 ft. 2 inches). He was born in Corsica in 1769, and was commissioned as a second lieutenant at the age of 16.

579 William Joyce. An American who became a British citizen, he made propaganda broadcasts for Germany. He was found guilty of treason, and hanged.

580 Pizarro. He defeated the Incas in 1528, and ruled Peru until 1541 when he was assassinated.

Master brain 2

581 The amount an elastic body bends or stretches out of shape is in direct proportion to the force acting on it. 'A strain is proportional to the stress producing it.' Often expressed in the brief form 'Strain is proportional to stress'. The law applies as long as the body is still elastic. Increased stress beyond this elastic limit will change the shape of the body permanently.

582 It was a Plan officially known as 'The European Recovery Program' by which the U.S.A. encouraged European nations to work together for economic recovery. Aid was sent to European countries in the form of food, machinery and other products. George C. Marshall suggested the Plan; it began in April 1948 and ended in 1951.

583 Isle of Man. Title of the two justices of the common law courts of the Isle of Man. In Scotland, 'dempster' or 'doomster' was the name of the officer formerly attached to the high court of justiciary, who pronounced the doom or sentence on a condemned person. This office no longer persists.

584 Sweden received Norway from Denmark. This was in 1814/15 after the Napoleonic Wars.

585 Two groups of political parties who served in the legislative assembly. The *Mountain* (consisting of the Jacobins and Cordeliers) were in the highest part of the hall on the speaker's left. The *Plain* (consisting of more conservative members) were in the low central section and to the right of the speaker.

Some historians believe that the 'left' and 'right' used as terms for political parties was derived from this.

586 The ordinary soldiers who fought on each side. 'Johnny Reb' was the southerner or the Confederate soldier. 'Billy Yank' was the northerner or Union or Federal soldier.

587 He used a bridge of boats. Xerxes I was the King of Persia and continued the war against Greece. He used a double line of ships to form a bridge across the Hellespont across which his vast army marched.

588 These were attacks on the toll-gates in west Wales by men who dressed as women. The riots are associated with the discontent expressed in the towns by the Chartist Movement. There was bitter dissatisfaction with the Poor Law Amendment Act of 1834.

589 In the Underwriting Room at Lloyd's, the big insurance market. One stroke meant bad news, two strokes meant good news to follow. The bell has a variety of uses. One is to inform the Underwriting Room of arrivals of overdue vessels. The bell is *not* used to give information about a sinking ship. It is also used to call members to attention and to announce news, e.g. *Apollo* flight, visit by Prime Minister, etc.

The bell belonged to the British frigate *Lutine* which was wrecked on 9 October 1799 off the coast of Holland. It was carrying a cargo of gold bullion insured at Lloyd's. It was a total loss.

590 They were the first words transmitted on the first successful telephone. Alexander Graham Bell was about to test a new transmitter. His assistant, Thomas A. Watson, waited in another room. Bell spilled some acid from a battery on his clothes. He cried out, 'Mr Watson, come here. I want you!' Watson rushed in, shouting that he had heard every word.

591 1. Jane Seymour. 2. Anne Boleyn.

592 The trip of the Moon around the Earth. The time from new Moon to new Moon is longer (29 days 12 hours 44 minutes 2·8 seconds) because the Earth moves around the Sun.

593 The planets move in elliptical orbits with the Sun at one focus. Three laws of planetary motion were published by Johannes Kepler, the German astronomer, in the 1600s.

594 In the Country of the Blind. *The Country of the Blind* is one of H. G. Wells' famous short stories. An explorer, Nunez, comes upon a strange country where everyone is blind. He finds that he is considered the deprived person, and is not acceptable until he gets rid of his sight.

   H. G. Wells quotes the 16th century proverb frequently: 'In the Country of the Blind the One-eyed Man is King.'

595 1. A donkey. 2. Robert Louis Stevenson. From his book *Travels with a donkey in the Cevennes*.

596 Tritium. More technically, the mass of an atom of deuterium is about twice that of a normal hydrogen atom.

597 King Philip II of Spain. King William I, Prince of Orange, brought together the northern provinces of the Netherlands in a league to defy King Philip who wanted to control the Low Countries and stamp out the Protestant religion there. For three years William the Silent escaped Philip's vengeance until an assassin killed him in 1584.

Speed Quiz 4

598 Horse chestnut.
599 Solomon.
600 Godiva.
601 Water.
602 William Shakespeare.
603 Amphibians.
604 A watt.
605 Goldilocks.
606 Oasis. They vary from small clumps of trees to fertile areas covering several hundred square miles.
607 Vote.
608 Gives up his throne.
609 A red rose.
610 At the bottom of the sea.
611 'La Gioconda' or the wife of Francesco del Giocondo.
612 Amerigo Vespucci. He claimed to have discovered America in 1497. In 1507 South America was named after 'Amerigo', then the name was adopted for North America as well.
613 Oxygen. Red lead is triplumbic tetroxide, Pb_3O_4, also called minimum.
614 Spanish.
615 40, recalling Christ's 40 days' fast in the wilderness.
616 A mahout.
617 A prison van or police van.

Geography

618 Tasmania.
619 Canada. The 'Mounties' are the Royal Canadian Mounted Police.
620 To see the bulb fields.
621 The sea bed, bordering the continents, which is covered by shallow water. Beyond the continental shelf there is

a sudden drop in the sea bed, giving a steep, cliff-like
edge referred to as the continental slope.

622 Urals.

623 The elevated land (or the boundary line) separating the
headstreams which are tributary to different river
systems and basins.

624 Liechtenstein.

625 The streams and rivers that flow to the great oceans,
the Atlantic and the Pacific, The Continental Divide is
the great ridge of the Rocky Mountain summits.

626 Bangladesh and Burma.

627 Coffee, Sao Paulo is Brazil's largest city.

628 Skagerrak, about 130 miles long.

629 Kariba Dam.

630 Because there are so many Buddhist priests to be seen
there, all wearing their yellow or saffron robes.

631 9 o'clock in the evening. Tokyo is eight hours ahead of
British Standard Time.

632 Tristan da Cunha. The islanders were evacuated to
Britain, and most of them returned to the island in 1963.

633 Moscow. A kopeck is a copper coin worth about ½p.
Gorki Park is Moscow's most popular amusement centre.

634 Jurassic limestone.

General Knowledge 9

635 They were crowned with wreaths of laurel. They were
also sometimes awarded wreaths of wild olives, green
parsley and green pine leaves.

636 Cirrus.

637 They have one or more long hairlike projections from
their bodies, known as flagella, which they whip about
rapidly. Flagellates are one-celled creatures, some plant-
like and some animal-like; a class of 'protozoa'.

638 1. On Croagh Patrick Mountain (a holy mountain in
Mayo). 2. To celebrate the banishing by St Patrick of

all reptiles from Ireland, which is traditionally supposed
to have happened here.

639 Laika.

640 The Law. They are barristers or training to be barristers.
Students apply to one of the four Inns, and attend
courses arranged by the Council of Legal Education.
They must dine at the Inn a certain number of times
during the terms that they keep.

641 *Santa Maria*. It was Columbus's flagship.

642 White stars of low overall light output, small size and
very great density.

643 About 44 feet . . . because the gravitation of the Moon
is about a sixth of that on Earth. Fosbury should
therefore be able to jump about six times higher.

644 Far off or distant. Derived from the Greek *tele*
meaning 'far off'.

645 Isadora Duncan, 1878–1927.

646 'Depth of field' is the depth of the region in which
objects will be in focus. It is dependent upon the aperture
of the lens. 'Exposure' means the total amount of light
reaching the film. This is controlled by the shutter speed
and the aperture of the lens.

647 The atom bomb. Fermi was the physicist who designed
the first atomic piles and produced the first nuclear
chain reaction in 1942. He worked on the atomic bomb
project in Los Alamos, U.S.A., and won the Nobel
Prize in physics for his atomic research.

648 An independent country in Western Africa. It is landlocked between Mali, Niger, Dahomey, Togo, Ghana
and the Ivory Coast. Formerly French, Upper Volta
became an independent republic in August 1960. Its
official name is Republique de Haute Volta.

649 It is a river pilot term meaning two fathoms (a depth
of 12 feet). Samuel Langhorne Clemens was a river
pilot on the Mississippi.

The drawings for the picture quizzes are taken from books in the *Picture Reference* series, published by Brockhampton Press.

Picture Reference books are designed to provide authentic and accurate background material for use in many ways – at home, in the library and at school; and in particular to form the basis of one's own reference library. Each book has about 300 photographs and line drawings, and the illustrations are taken from original sources.

STAMP COLLECTING

Stanley Phillips

The Stanley Gibbons standard work on stamp collecting, now for the first time in paperback. Revised and brought up-to-date with new material and with 16 pages of photographs.

Contents include: The story of the post – stamp designing and printing – overprints – colours – postmarks – forgeries – the outfit – how to get and identify stamps – arranging the collection – different kinds of collection – the stamp world – treasure trove.

With an appendix covering stamp currencies – philatelic terms in three languages – stamp inscriptions translated – the meaning of overprints.

These are other Knight Books

Falcon Travis

CAMPING AND HIKING

This is a new book – written, designed and
illustrated to be a guide for anyone who is
going camping or hiking, whether alone, with
a few friends, or in a larger party.

From equipment and personal gear to striking
camp and packing up at the end, there is
something of interest to everyone, however
experienced they are. The extra material
covers many vital and fascinating aspects of
life in the country – maps and compasses, knives
and axes, first aid, logs and nature diaries,
weather and safety precautions.

The book is published with the support and approval
of the Scout Association, and covers almost all the
tests for the Scout Standard and Advanced Scout
Standard.

These are other Knight Books

FIRST BBC TV TOP OF THE FORM QUIZ BOOK

SECOND BBC TV TOP OF THE FORM QUIZ BOOK

FOURTH BBC TV TOP OF THE FORM QUIZ BOOK

FIFTH BBC TV TOP OF THE FORM QUIZ BOOK

More 'Top of the Form' quiz books, all compiled by the programme's Question Setter, Boswell Taylor, and containing over 700 questions and full answers on dozens of different subjects.

Falcon Travis

FIRST KNIGHT BOOK OF PUZZLES
SECOND KNIGHT BOOK OF PUZZLES
THIRD KNIGHT BOOK OF PUZZLES
FOURTH KNIGHT BOOK OF PUZZLES

Everything for the puzzle enthusiast – word, picture and number puzzles, general knowledge quizzes, crosswords with a difference, secret codes, and lots of new puzzles which you won't have come across before.

These birds' names have got split up. Can you put them together again? Bill hatch, Jack finch, Mag pipit, Spoon tree, Nut pie, Daw haw.

The answer to this riddle is an anagram of
LURELAMB

Though not its proper function,
Said its owner, Henry Tupp,
It might go up a chimney down,
But never down one up.

The vowels are missing from these words. Can you discover them, with the help of the clues?

   K   A tree
  RB   Breed of horse
RWG   Insect

Which two odd numbers, when multiplied together, give 7 as the answer?

Two men are sitting facing each other in a railway compartment with the window open. The train enters a tunnel and a puff of sooty smoke blackens the face of one of them. When the train comes out of the tunnel the man with the clean face goes out to wash, but the one with the sooty face does not. Why?

You'll find the answers to these and lots of similar questions, including picture questions, in *First Knight Book of Puzzles* compiled by Falcon Travis, a White Knight Book.

Primrose Cumming
FOUR RODE HOME

Two boys and two girls plan a holiday with a
difference – a riding tour across southern
England from the New Forest back home to Kent.
They intend to stay at youth hostels overnight,
and to keep to bridle-paths, quiet lanes and open
ground while on the move, but it doesn't always
work out that way.

Charles M. Schultz

MEET THE PEANUTS GANG

DON'T TREAD ON CHARLIE BROWN

WHAT WERE YOU SAYING,
CHARLIE BROWN?

If you haven't met the Peanuts gang before, now's
your chance to get acquainted with Charlie
Brown and his friends (not forgetting Snoopy the
dog) who have made such a hit in this country
and the United States. And if you are already a
Peanuts fan, these books contain some of the
earlier cartoons which you probably won't have
seen before.

These are other Knight Books

Rene Guillot

THREE GIRLS AND A SECRET

Michele and Manuela live in Paris and have a very big secret – they have furnished a flat in a row of houses soon to be demolished. They visit their 'home' whenever they can, accompanied by Ajax, a stray Alsatian dog who loves the two girls but nearly gets them into trouble through his skill in stealing handbags. Ajax was the one who discovered their second big secret – an abandoned baby which the girls take back to the flat with the intention of looking after him for just one day. But when one of their friends, Caroline, sees the baby, she wants to keep him and look after him, and then the problems begin.

Illustrated by Jane Paton

John Buchan

THE THREE HOSTAGES

Further adventures of Richard Hannay, hero of *The Thirty Nine Steps*, this thrilling story is set in the period of the First World War. It tells of an assignment full of suspense, mystery, intrigue and danger.

THE FOREST OF BOLAND LIGHT RAILWAY
'*BB*'

One of the most famous and popular of modern fantasies, now in paperback for the first time as a result of public demand

The Forest of Boland Light Railway with its magnificent steam engine, the *Boland Belle*, is the pride and joy of the gnomes who live in the Forest. But one day their enemies the leprechauns overcome the gnomes in a surprise attack, and drag them off to their stronghold, Castle Shera. The outlook seems bleak, but the cowzies come to the rescue just in time.

Ask your local bookseller, or at your public library, for details of other Knight Books, or write to the Editor-in-Chief, Knight Books, Arlen House, Salisbury Road, Leicester LE1 7QS